THE
RIPPLE
EFFECT

First published in the UK in 2023 by
Black & White Publishing Ltd
Nautical House, 104 Commercial Street, Edinburgh, EH6 6NF

A division of Bonnier Books UK
4th Floor, Victoria House, Bloomsbury Square, London, WC1B 4DA
Owned by Bonnier Books
Sveavägen 56, Stockholm, Sweden

This book is based in part on interviews about the lives and experiences of its
contributors. In some cases names have been changed solely to protect the privacy of
others. The authors have stated to the publishers that the contents of these interviews
are true and accurate to the best of their knowledge.

The Ripple Effect isn't a guide to swimming safety and therefore neither the
authors nor the publisher can accept any responsibility for damage of any kind, to
property or persons, that occurs either directly or indirectly from the use of this book or
from any wild swimming activity.

A CIP catalogue record for this book is available from the British Library.

ISBN: 978 1 78530 471 2

1 3 5 7 9 10 8 6 4 2

Layout by Black & White Publishing
Printed and bound in Lithuania

FSC
www.fsc.org
MIX
Paper from
responsible sources
FSC® C107574

www.blackandwhitepublishing.com

THE RIPPLE EFFECT

A Celebration of Britain's Brilliant Wild Swimming Communities

Anna Deacon & Vicky Allan

BLACK & WHITE PUBLISHING

To all the Tits, Balls and Wild Ones
of our beloved Edinburgh beaches.

THE RIPPLE EFFECT

CHAPTER 1

THE WILD ONES

THE SWIM COMMUNITY IN MICROCOSM

It starts with a ripple. Everything does. A ripple, a disturbance, the beat of a butterfly's wing.

Back in 2018, when what we call the originals gathered on our local Wardie Bay beach, there would generally be no more than ten hardy folk, often laughed at by others who would shake their heads and declare, "You'd never catch me doing that."

Four years later, in the run-up to Christmas 2022, there were hundreds – all pitched up for a charity swim in aid of the local hospice. The bakes were selling like hot cakes, a queue trailed halfway down the beach to buy raffle tickets and a herd of ecstatic figures, dressed in Santa hats and baubles, thundered and squealed into the water.

It seems grandiose to talk about the wild swimming movement – isn't a movement normally a matter of rights? – but the word fits with what we see out there. A ripple, a wave, a movement.

When, in 2019, we published our first swimming book, *Taking the Plunge*, we joked that we were lucky to have caught the peak of what seemed like a small wild swimming wave. Then Covid hit, and the wave swelled. We looked around and there were more groups, more Bluetits, Blue Balls, Menopausal Mermaids, Polar Bears, Selkies, Salty Sisters, Blue Flamingos, Salty Seabirds, Salty Grief Warriors, Bob & Blether, Out of Sink Synchro Swimmers. There were names that made us chuckle – names that said something about the daft and playful wild swimming world we knew.

So, yes, let's call it a movement. And let's also call that movement joy. Because – when we look at what all the different groups have in common – that's what we see. It's joy laced with a bit of inner child.

What's striking, too, is that wild swimming doesn't exist in isolation. In these group names, we can see many other movements expressed. Each chapter of this book tells one of their stories. Menopause awareness, mental health, body positivity, sobriety, male mental health. There are even, in our Dawnstalkers chapter, ripples of climate awareness and eco-anxiety.

We also began to see, as we looked at our groups, how many of swimming's benefits weren't strictly the physiological effects that have now been much researched. It's not all about diving into the cold – it's about doing it together, in company, and supporting each other all the way through.

That's why, early on in writing this book, we asked one of our heroes, Dr Rangan Chatterjee, the big question: "Is it the

> "We have found a wonderful little community of similarly mad people, always friendly, warm and welcoming. Together we have shivered, made snow angels, danced, cast spells, laughed and cried; we have bobbed in the water, been dunked by the waves, we have even swum to all the buoys, and picked up what feels like tons of rubbish."
>
> **Fiona Hamilton, Murrayfield Mermaids**

swimming, or is it the community?"

"It's a bit of both," he said, "but I think the community is probably the biggest thing."

Rangan recalled how Nick Pearson, the CEO of Parkrun, once told him, "Parkrun is a social intervention masquerading as a running event." That idea, he said, had stayed with him – that there was something important in socially coming together to exercise. "I think," he said, "community is the missing piece in health."

In the following pages you will find many people reflecting on that question and pondering what it is about swimming together that can be so transformational – as well as those who simply celebrate and describe what it is and what it feels like.

We start, in this chapter, with one beach – the city bay on which Anna first began swimming, before there was anything like a community frequenting it, when there was only the faintest ripple of wild swimming on its shore.

This beach was our jumping board, our platform from which to dive off, as we started to explore the patchwork of communities at our shorelines. For it seemed to us that this tiny city beach contained all the pieces, all those different movements, in a microcosm.

In this one small bay we found so many types of groups, all using the same stretch of sand. There were skinny dippers, ice warriors, mental health swimmers and moon worshippers. There were fundraisers and coaches. All of wild swimming life seemed to be there.

THE WARDIE BAY WILD ONES

ANNA'S STORY

I moved to Edinburgh in 2016 and our new home was only a five-minute walk from the sea. When we explored the area, we discovered a little harbour with a beach next to it. Most days I went walking there. It is great for sea glass, seabirds and seals, and not regularly cleaned or cared for by the local authority, which meant alongside the nature there was often a lot of sea-borne litter.

However, aside from the odd dog walker, I rarely saw anyone there. Hidden from the road which runs alongside it, the beach is sheltered by a long breakwater and grows and shrinks enormously with the tide. The views across the Firth of Forth to Fife are punctuated by a little island half-way across. This became my patch; I litter picked, I ran, I beachcombed, and I started to consider swimming, although, as I had never seen anyone swimming there, I was too nervous to attempt it as it was such an unknown quantity.

A little later, I joined a swimming group called the Wild Ones who met at a much larger beach, Portobello, further east along the coast, after seeing some intrepid swimmers exit the water on a freezing cold day onto icy sand. I knew I wanted to do that too.

It reminded me of hilariously cold swims in the Highlands with my sister through my childhood, and teenage skinny dips in frozen lochs and the wondrous rush of adrenaline and joy I felt afterwards. I swam as much as I could with my cousin, who was already a seasoned all-year-round swimmer, but it wasn't always possible to meet up and I wanted to swim more regularly.

The group seemed very friendly when they chatted on Facebook, but I couldn't pluck up the courage to actually go and meet them in real life. Then one day someone mentioned Wardie Bay and asked if anyone had swum there. There was a handful of us who replied saying we would love to try, and so we met in late summer 2018 for the first Wardie Bay swim. None of us knew anyone, so we were all in the same boat; there were about eight of us on that first swim and we decided to meet every Sunday at the same time. The Wardie Wild Ones group was born.

People always stopped and stared incredulously at us, asked us if we were mad, if we were going to freeze in there. But often people would say they have always fancied a sea swim and could they join us. Our group grew slowly but surely, we invited friends along to try it out and, by the end of 2019 we had probably around fifty people in our Facebook group and regular weekend dip times and a few midweek sessions too. We celebrated birthdays on the shore with little beach fires and birthday cakes, we had dressing-up swims at Easter, Christmas and solstices, we had loony dooks on New Year's Day, night swims, adventured elsewhere as a group to try new places, and we often met up with the Wild Ones group down in Portobello, joining them for social evenings and big swims.

When the Covid pandemic struck, our community, like so many others, was displaced. You couldn't swim together, so many people started swimming alone, or just not swimming at all. As we were stuck in our local area, more people started to visit the beach. And the beautiful weather at the beginning of lockdown made the prospect of a sea swim so enticing, and so the number of swimmers at our little beach began to grow. As restrictions eased off, small groups formed, new swimmers brought friends along and bit by bit everything changed.

We now have a vibrant community of over three thousand swimmers in our Facebook group, with more joining all the time, and now the beach nearly always has a little pod of swimmers on it.

Many smaller groups formed through the pandemic now meet regularly for swims. A big community fundraiser swim at Christmas raised money for the local hospice, St Columba's; a large gathering took part in a summer solstice yoga session followed by a dip; there are swim teachers giving regular classes to improve your open water strokes; a sunrise skinny dip group; a mental health swimming group . . . and so much more. Money raised from dip-a-day charity swims and other charity swim events goes to local charities, and regular beach cleans take place as swimmers are keen to look after their patch. All these friendships and connections that spread beyond the water mean that the ripple effect from this small beach out to the local community is really being felt.

And this is just our tiny local beach. A similar ripple is also being felt right across the UK and beyond as wild swimming grows and with it a swell of wellbeing, friendships and, most of all, community.

What goes on at the beach is an extension of the local community. There are so many stories I could tell of people I have met and of connections forged through swimming. Here is just one that says so much about the web that exists between the beach and the city.

In 2019 my darling granny was receiving end-of-life care in a local care home, which is where I went to show her the very first copy of *Taking the Plunge*. Granny was a photographer, too, and for me to show her a book of my photographs was a real moment; she was able to hold it and look through it with me and it meant the world to me to share that with her. She sadly died, with us at her side, the day the book was published. I will always remember the amazing staff who cared for her; in particular Angela, who gave my dear granny such care and would always lift her spirits and make her laugh. It was clear that Angela was a very special human being.

I didn't want to leave Granny on her own after she passed, but Angela gave me a hug and said she would stay with her until the undertakers arrived, so she wasn't alone. That small act of kindness meant so much to us as a family and we were deeply touched when she attended the funeral, too.

The next time I saw Angela was on the beach around a year or two later: she had a small group of women with her, and we ran to each other for a huge hug. She had read the copy of *Taking the Plunge* that I'd left in the care home with Granny and had decided to give swimming a go during lockdown. The incredible warmth Angela showed to our family and my granny was right there on the beach. She has inspired so many people to the water and has become something of the mother hen to a group of women that just keeps growing: they are always laughing, always having fun.

THE MOTHER HEN
ANGELA WEIR

Family Weir

I met Anna at the care home I worked in when she was in the process of having *Taking the Plunge* published, and I can remember going home and telling my daughter Eilidh all about it and how we should try it. She was reluctant, having been brought up primarily in the Middle East and Southeast Asia. She was used to warmer water.

A couple of months down the line and my (now) ex-husband decided he didn't want to be with "this" anymore, as he pointed to my body! He had always been critical of my weight gain throughout our marriage, but I hadn't realised it was that bad. This was the spur I needed and, having read up on wild swimming, I thought I had nothing to lose. I persuaded Eilidh to join me and off we went down to Wardie. I couldn't believe it and was hooked from the first swim. Eilidh managed to get in up to her thighs.

A couple of Eilidh's friends joined us and, slowly but surely, the Pod was starting to form, growing from three to thirty-six. People have approached us on the beach and asked to join, people have sent random

messages and asked to join.

I find that there is no judgement, no body shaming, and I have never felt conscious of my size down at Wardie. It has done so much for my body confidence and my general confidence and, on those down days, you just swim a wee bit further out and have a wee cry. The water soothes and holds me, and I go home feeling ready for anything.

It really is the best thing I have ever done, and I can't imagine not doing it. Thank you, Anna – and, of course, wee Granny Pat – because you are the ones who started my journey.

THE FUNDRAISERS
ALEX CLARKE

St Columba's Dook A Day

My serious cold swimming journey started after I had just had my third son and my marriage had sadly failed. It was in the latter stages of the lockdown, when Wardie Bay became our new community hub for like-minded dookers. My good friend Colleen and I saved every Sunday morning for our cold escape, which provided me with a sanctuary of support during the most horrendous stage of my life.

We started in wetsuits, but then soon took the move to swimmers, swimming through two years of freezing temps, and have never looked back. I still remember that first sensation of body numbness and Colleen having fits of giggles.

I was lucky to start volunteering for the events fundraising team at St Columba's hospice care, which overlooks Wardie Bay,

and one of the first events they needed help with was Dook A Day in May. It felt like the perfect opportunity for me to start in this new field of work. We were able to create a wonderful group of women who, often for personal reasons, felt the real push to do this daily challenge while raising over £19,000 for the hospice!

I found it incredibly demanding and exhausting as my baby was still little. But the camaraderie and support that we gave each other in person and on our group chat was priceless. In October 2022, I was lucky enough to secure a post as a community fundraiser and have been involved in lots of fundraisers down on the beach. I hope to make Dook A Day even bigger and better in 2023 and beyond.

ANDRE PHILLIPS

Papyrus fundraiser

Wardie Bay community was central to my 2022 adventure to swim a hundred kilometres around Arran. When I was first thinking about doing it, most people said, "That's mad, it can't be possible right?" Not the Wardie Bay Wild Ones: "Oh that sounds fantastic, you should chat to X or Y, they've done big swims!"

Hours of training at Wardie saw lots of enthusiasm for my adventure, which was so sorely needed. I also got all my coaching from Debbie Kelso, a regular coach down at Wardie, without which I certainly wouldn't have completed the swim. In memory of a friend from Arran, I raised over £7,500 for Papyrus, a teenage mental health charity.

THE ICE WOMAN
COLLEEN REEVE

creator of Ice Women Edinburgh and yoga instructor

The cold water was something that I never used to be into at all. My husband would swim with the boys, and I would stand and watch the bags. I wasn't a very confident swimmer and didn't like getting wet or cold. Then, during lockdown, we were bored, and the weather was nice, so we started going down to Wardie Bay and giving it a go in our wetsuits. I loved seeing how joyous and exhilarated the boys were and they encouraged me to join in, so I did!

Then, in the winter, I started going with my neighbour who had just had a new baby. We went every Sunday morning at 8 a.m. At first, we wore wetsuits, but by spring we braved it in our swimsuits. I loved it and I used to get the giggles when I came out. I think it must have been the endorphin rush.

I was also amazed that there were so many women there at Wardie Bay. It didn't seem like anyone was very body conscious. Everyone was there in their swimsuits, and it felt like an inclusive community.

I've been doing yoga for quite a long time, and I've had some wonderful experiences at yoga studios but, if I'm honest,

I think we have a long way to go to make yoga truly inclusive. Also, maybe when you go to a yoga class you don't really talk to anyone there. That's okay, but this was different. This was women coming together and literally baring all; being open and chatty, and no one was competing about how long they'd been in. I liked that.

We then formed a little Wardie Bay WhatsApp group with some other women, and we started to swim together. There was a feeling of camaraderie between us, a friendliness and supportiveness. It felt good.

I started doing some research into cold water swimming and read Wim Hof's book. I was interested in the breathing exercises he was doing because of the similarity to pranayama, which is breathwork in yoga. Learning how to use your breath is such a powerful tool. You can use it to calm yourself down when you're going into the cold water. It helps you to simply be and to allow it to happen, not fight against it. It is empowering. You think, "Wow, I can do this." It makes you feel strong, and I wanted to share that.

I was also inspired by Wim Hof because he had tragically lost his wife and had used the cold to help heal himself. My dad had died suddenly before Covid. It happened when my son was in hospital, so it was quite a traumatic time and I struggled to process everything. I was trying hard to stay busy and be a good mum, a good daughter, a good teacher, and so on, but the feeling was very raw.

Every time I did yoga and meditated, I cried because the sadness was always there, underneath the surface. I lost my sister when I was eleven, and when you experience something like that, the grief never really goes away. Losing poor Dad brought it all back.

That doesn't mean I wasn't happy. I met Chris when I was eighteen and he brings me so much happiness, as do my boys and all my family. I have lots to be happy about. Grief can co-exist with happiness and it's not always a bad thing; but it's always there. Yet when I went into the cold water, I found a sense of relief. It was like the waves washed it all away. I had to stop and breathe and feel the sensations in my body, the tingling on my skin. Nothing else brings the body, the breath and the mind together so intensely.

Dr Bessel van der Kolk – author of *The Body Keeps the Score: Mind, Brain and Body in the Transformation of Trauma* – believes that emotions are physical sensations, and that the body quite literally keeps the score and gets stuck in past trauma. He encourages movement, particularly yoga, as a way of healing because it helps you to reconnect with your body and to be more aware of how the body reacts with the physical world around it.

When you submerge yourself in cold water, it's impossible to ignore how your body feels!

Interestingly, Bessel van der Kolk also believes that being part of a group doing something physical together helps with recovery from trauma because it helps you to re-establish your capacity to connect with those around you. It's almost the idea of healing in communities, like a kind of social prescribing.

His ideas got me thinking about how I could combine teaching yoga with cold water therapy and create a community around that. So, I set up Wild Yoga Scotland and started teaching weekly yoga and breathwork classes on the beach, which included an optional dip at the end. I had only ever taught in a studio, so I was quite nervous, but the women who came seemed to like it and it felt good, so I kept going.

As the summer turned into autumn and it started to get colder, I thought that my classes would come to a natural end. But then I read Susanna Søberg's book, *Winter Swimming: The Nordic Way Towards a Healthier and Happier Life*, and I thought if there's ever a time to do it, it should be now. So, I launched my winter yoga and swim classes and was surprised that people signed up. I had to change what I would usually teach to make it enjoyable. It's not that pleasurable to do yoga outside in the winter in Scotland with no socks or shoes on: it's freezing!

I adapted the sequence so we could do it standing and wear trainers and warm jackets. I wanted us to flow in rhythm with our breath and with one another, and to feel the warmth that we could generate in our bodies. Then we braved the cold water, and that small experience of adversity had the power to bring the group together. Being outside in winter, moving and breathing together, warming up afterwards by dancing, drinking tea and eating flapjacks; it felt like we had created something new, something that made us feel good. And that's the power of the cold water.

THE DOCTOR
DR SUZY SCARLETT
Ice Women

I've always had an interest in living a healthy lifestyle and trying to find balance in the two most obvious pillars – nutrition and physical activity. This isn't always easy in your early medical career or with young children, but once everyone was sleeping through the night again and I finished my GP training, I was needing more from my job. I realised that I was becoming a transactional GP, sticking on plasters so to speak, without going to the root cause. I was then introduced to the British Society of Lifestyle Medicine, and I studied for the diploma during the first year of lockdown. This took me (and my family) on our own lifestyle journey first, and since then I have used this knowledge, experience and techniques in my everyday practice, in my teaching, and in my regional diabetes role too.

We live in a society that is making us sick; an environment that is designed for convenience, where food is available at every corner, movement is optional, and comfort is king, but as human beings we are not designed for this. Our busy lifestyles are full of stresses, so we're constantly pumping out stress hormones into our system, getting us ready for fight or flight. We need to slow down and find an antidote to all of this.

Part of the answer for me is cold water swimming, in my case cautiously, among a community of likeminded folk. Why? Owing to the myriad of physical and mental health

benefits: the initial cold shock soon gives way to a sense of release and peaceful-ness, as the physiological effects of fight or flight are taken over by endorphins. Done repeatedly, the body begins to adapt to this stress response and can replicate it in the context of unrelated daily stresses. I've certainly noticed a drop in my migraine frequency since starting dipping, and I can use my swimming to release the tension I carry in my neck and shoulder muscles after a week of the work-life-mum juggle.

I recall sharing a picture of a group of "brave souls sampling the North Sea" in the autumn before lockdown on social media – and thinking they were bonkers. Months later I saw a neighbour emerging from the surf and she encouraged me to give it a go. Maybe, I thought, if she could, I could. So, one sunny winter's day I dipped my toe in, literally. Then my feet. Another time I went up to my knees and decided I could. I dusted off my wetsuit and found some gloves, got some top tips like wrapping my towel in a hot water bottle for afterwards, and joined a friend who had been doing it for ages. I abso-lutely loved it, I was hooked. Lately I've been lucky enough to join a wonderfully supportive group of Ice Women, led by Colleen Reeve of Wild Yoga Scotland. Outdoor yoga first, then a walk and a talk, breathwork, then a swim. It's always hard getting in, but so much easier in the com-pany of others. Accountability like that is hard to beat.

THE CHANNEL SWIMMER
TINE BARKMAN
the Shiver Club

It's fair to say that Wardie Bay has completely changed my life path. We moved to Edinburgh on the last weekend in February 2020, a few weeks before the first lockdown, and arrived in a new city which then immediately shut down. So, in lockdown, we started to explore our surroundings and Wardie Bay is within walking distance. I remember thinking, every time I passed by, "This is the first time in my life I have lived within walking distance of a beach. I wonder if people swim here?"

Then spring came and with it the evidence that people did indeed swim at Wardie Bay. On the first weekend in June 2020, it was warm, the water was crystal clear, and I jumped in for the first time. I was greeted by the amazing swim community, which at that point started growing. After that, Wardie Bay became my second home.

Eventually, I thought, swimming has always been a part of my life, why not take it a bit further and get coached sessions? Which is how I met Colin. My job then was as a trekking guide for a German company. Owing to the pandemic, that job had disappeared. I swam a few times with Colin before he suggested that he could actually use an assistant coach and asked if I wanted to become one. And I thought, "Hm, there is an idea, why not?"

Lockdown struck again and, before I could get my qualification in May 2021,

I swam through a different adventure: my first winter! Suddenly it was December, January, February, and we were still swimming. It was easy! That is how the Shiver Club was born, five of us meeting four times a week to shiver through winter together. Three of us still do.

In 2022, a friend of mine and I swam the Channel in a relay with Wardie Bay being our training ground. I'm completely convinced that without the constant motivation and smiles from everybody at the beach, not to mention the help with bake sales for our fundraiser, I would not have swum to France. Wardie Bay made that happen.

> "A friend, Eve, convinced me to sea swim with her for the first time 'because it's Halloween, a full moon and too weird not to'. It's three and a half years later and I'm in every week. In Eve's wise words, 'You never regret a swim, so just GET IN THE SEA!'"
>
> **Lucy Neville**

THE ANTI-SEWAGE CAMPAIGNER
SUSIE READE

Wardie Bay 4 Bathing Waters Status campaigner

I'm not a campaigner by nature, held back by confusion when filling in forms and difficulty with selecting vocabulary which might convey knowledge and certainty. But friends with many skills supported this application – for Bathing Waters status – from the start. It seemed obvious to me that water testing was needed, not just for bathing but, primarily, for the health of the water and diversity of wildlife. Thirty years ago, I took my children swimming in the Firth of Forth, among the condoms and tampons. Thankfully, sewage management has improved hugely since then but it's not a vote-catcher, so is underfunded. Finally, after three years of campaigning, in 2023, our little beach at Wardie has been designated a "Bathing Water". That feels wonderful, but it is just a beginning.

For a few months each year, it will be tested for levels of key bacteria and an electronic sign will provide us with information about the water quality. From here we can focus our next step.

I would not have got anywhere at all

without marine campaigner Karen Bates, who is not a swimmer, but who understands campaigning and political manoeuvring and is extremely knowledgeable. As I write this, the rain is pouring down in Italy, which reminds me of my convincement – a Quaker noun – that we should be responsible for the medium in which we live and not take it for granted. That includes the water, the air, the earth, the plants, the fungus, the animals.

These media have processes which we must support by keeping the environmental balance but avoiding wasteful use of resources. Human lifecycles rely on them being healthy. Children must be able to explore the environment playfully and grow well. Adults must be able to use surrounding spaces to enjoy social life. All these meandering thoughts are what fuel my swimming at Wardie with my little group of swim chums.

THE BLUETIT
HELEN O'DONNELL

Edinburgh Bluetits

I rediscovered the joy of swimming in the sea during lockdown. I grew up in South Queensferry, where we spent many hours jumping off the Hawes pier or playing on the beach we called "the Shell Beds"; I now know it was Peatdraught Bay we were playing on.

In Oct 2020, I was lying in bed, quite low, scrolling through Facebook, when I came across the Bluetit Chill Swimmers page. They looked so much fun and my kind of people. Every time I see the logo, which is so bright and cheery, I can't help but smile.

Lockdown was pretty tough. Like many therapists, I found myself listening to others' experience of an event I was simultaneously going through myself. My relationship at the time was also challenging, not supportive, and wild swimming was definitely not something she supported.

Establishing the Edinburgh Bluetits was my antidote. It brought balance back to my life. It's where I laughed and played. Playing is so important, so good for my/our mental wellbeing, and yet as adults we tend not to do it, or worse, scoff at it. I love playing!

I spent hours on Wardie Bay flying our little flag. A flag is a very easy way to be found, especially as the beach got busier and busier. Such a contrast to the hours I have spent on Wardie Bay beach alone, enjoying the peace, the sound of the waves and the odd hello from a passer-by pre-Covid.

Lockdown put us all into little bubbles and, for many, isolation. Edinburgh Bluetits created a way to reconnect, build new friendships and reduce this isolation. Slowly, yet steadily, as we moved out of lockdown our numbers grew, until my favourite swim of the week was our Friday evening swim, blether and biscuits. I loved watching women (because it was mainly women at the start) challenge themselves in so many ways.

There was lots of nonsense and playfulness. Full moon swims in fancy dress, with bonfires, bacon rolls, cake (so much cake), chatter and laughter. Jumping in big woohoo waves and handstands. For our first birthday, one of our members taught a group of us a synchronised swim routine on the grass, then into the sea. Hilarious.

THE THERAPIST
DOUGLAS NICHOLSON

About five years ago, in March, I decided on a whim that I was going to swim. In the sea. At Edinburgh's scruffy little scrap of sand at Wardie Bay. The cold northerly was bringing in rain and four-foot waves. The fact there were some other people there is the only reason I got in. They were shouting and laughing, jumping the waves and body surfing like the world was about to end and this was their last chance to have some fun. Afterwards I got out, shivered my way home . . . and then glowed. Inside and out. I have been back pretty much every week since. Summer or winter, sun or snow. I now have a group of stalwart friends with whom I share this weekly experience.

I stress the people part because it is, for me and I think most others, an essential part of it. As humans, we love to share our experiences. We love to laugh at each other's squeals as we get in and then gossip through the immediate afterglow. Would you go on your own to a funfair? You might. And you would have fun. But probably not as much fun as you would with a gaggle of equally scared pals.

Perhaps because I'm a psychotherapist I wonder about the mood-enhancing effects of cold water swimming. When I was training, I remember seeing the drawings of workers at Victorian asylums locking patients into baths filled with freezing water.

What torture. And yet the benefits were clear: manic people calmed; depressed people made happier. As with electro-conclusive therapy, they had no idea how it worked. Just that it did. Nowadays we know that the body-stress of cold immersion triggers serotonin and dopamine production – exactly the same chemicals that are produced by antidepressants. But somehow, I feel it's not about the science, nor about the euphoric chemical production. It's more about peace, and beauty, and change, and mystery, and fellowship. These are the things that take me to "our little beach".

THE WARDIE BAY ORIGINAL GANGSTAS

KATHERINE HART

The sea swimming community, and Wardie in particular, is the first place I have truly felt "at home" since I moved to Edinburgh some sixteen years ago. Water seems to be a very special secret ingredient that brings people together. Our group may be small, but it is mighty. I've been astonished at the trust and friendships so quickly built and what we have shared in the water.

SANDRA RATHJEN

Wherever you swim, folks chat (often just a few words), help you out, and share experience and knowledge. The water is healing. Even during Covid – when lockdown released a little and we were able to get back in the water – seeing folk again, diving off the groynes when the water was deep enough, doing races and trips to far-flung East Lothian, such fun. But the best bit about the growth of the outdoor swimming community is that now many of my friends don't think I'm mad to swim all year round in a swimsuit, they've joined me!

PHILLIPA KEMP

Three years ago, I was looking over what felt like a cliff edge, following the end of a twenty-year marriage. My sister suggested two things that she thought would support me through what would inevitably be a turbulent period of my life. The first thing was to find an interest and the second was to build a community of friends around me. I had never bargained on finding both these things in one place.

Since around 2020, I've been part of a little group of wild swimmers based at Wardie: the Wardie Bay Original Gangstas, or WBOG! The group was started by a few intrepid swimmers, including Anna Deacon, who had begun swimming at the little urban beach long before the big explosion of wild swimming began. I'm a bit of a latecomer to the group to be considered one of the "originals", but it has become a lifeline for me and has helped me to literally and metaphorically navigate the turbulent waters of divorce, supporting one of my children through mental illness, moving house and changing jobs in the space of six months. I feel so lucky to have discovered it. I can't imagine a life without it.

RIPPLING BACK

In the years since Anna started swimming there, Wardie has changed. The site itself feels different, with its buzz of different people, like some leisure destination, though with still a little of the wild in it.

As a result of the Wardie Bay 4 Bathing Waters Status campaign, the bay now has bathing waters status; there is an electronic sign delivering regular information, throughout the summer, about the water quality. This too has felt like being part of a ripple, a wave. It has felt like being part of a movement which is about pushing for more monitoring of sewage release, not just for the health of swimmers, but for the sake of marine life too.

Wardie is, along its eighty-metre stretch, a version of the swimming world in miniature. What people do on this beach is reflected in swim spots all around the UK, and in groups hundreds of miles away. We know this because we have talked to them, and we heard the same stories.

They tell the same tales of synchronised swims and handstands; cake and bonfires; the comfort of having someone keep an eye out for you; the bond forged out on the water; and, above all, of friendship.

And at Wardie, as with so many other places, what is clear is that the beach, and the North Sea that washes it, and the people who swim in it, are not a detached entity. They are connected to a bigger community on the land. It's often said that what goes on in the sea stays in the sea.

But that's not entirely true. The ripples that start there spread. What's talked about and shared there washes back.

At Wardie we saw how a community grew and, with it, an impact on the world that the beach backs up against, a bustling, busy city.

We also saw how the swim community expanded in nearby Portobello, and how across the country it grew and grew, as more and more people came to the water.

And, as we talked more and more, we began to see its ripples. We thought, yes, there are ripples everywhere. And those ripples have become a torrent.

> *"Wild swimming helps me in menopause and helps me to wash away the pain. The sea heals me."*
>
> **Heather Holmyard**

CHAPTER 2

THE
BLUE BALLS

MEN SUPPORTING MEN

There was something special about this group – and it wasn't just that they were all men, unlike the mostly female swim-packs we had been seeing on beaches up to this point. It was the way that they stood on the sand in a circle, shifting from foot to foot, listening to each other, nodding and smiling. Each of them, one by one, taking turns to talk about how they are feeling, before they all charge, like an enthusiastic herd, into the water.

But then this was no ordinary swim group. This was the Edinburgh Blue Balls, a group explicitly about male mental health and with an Instagram strapline that declared: "Weekly cold water dip group to give men the chance to improve mental and physical health. Men supporting men."

Among those taking part in that pre-swim "check-in" in November 2021 was actor Johnny Panchaud, who recalled his very first such circle, vividly, as if he were still there.

"We're all standing on the sand, all these men of different shapes, sizes, ages. We're all nervous about swimming. And Marc, the founder of the group, says, 'We're going to do a check-in today.' Everyone was like, what the hell's a check-in? Normally getting in the water is the scary part.

"So, we're standing in a circle, and even that's scary, men getting in a circle, and we start telling each other how we're feeling and what we're struggling with. And these words like anxiety, depression, fear, things that people always experience but, especially men, never share, start coming out."

Johnny was, he told us, nearly fourteen months sober. Back in October 2020, he had hit a low. He had gone home to his parents' house, and, since they were away on holiday, found himself on his own with his thoughts. "I'm not going to say," he told me, "that I was thinking about committing suicide, because I don't think I would ever have had the bottle to see that through. But the thought had entered my mind for the first time, of how do I get out of this?"

He called an old friend in London who flew up "at the drop of a hat" and, after much chatting, he made a pledge to himself – he would stop drinking and taking recreational drugs.

Five days later, he took up an offer from friends to go for a "wild water swim" at Portobello. "It was something," he recalls, "that I would never do in a million years. I was the person walking down the beach saying you guys are mad, questioning their sanity."

In the run-up he found himself genuinely losing sleep over the imminent dip. "Having lived inside my comfort zone

"There have been a couple of times when lads were struggling and they've reached out. Seeing them being comfortable enough to open up and let us know, and seeing the other lads quickly offer support and help, showed me that we're doing something right."

**Chris Nicholas,
Ice Guys North East**

– because that's essentially what drinking and drugs is – to go and do something as bonkers as this was terrifying. I remember getting down there and it was dull, grey and miserable. The guys who were organising it were even umming and ahhing about whether we should go in. But we did it. I must have been in and out in two minutes, put my head under, screamed a little and then tiptoed back onto the beach. But after that, I don't know what it was, but I went religiously, every single day for one month."

In that early stage, he said, he was not "ready to look back at the trail of destruction I'd caused with my drinking and drugs". Nor was he ready to look forward. "I felt I've got to take this one day at a time. I've got to find a way of staying sober today. And with wild swimming, you physically can't think about anything other than now and survival."

NO LONGER ALONE

It's not hard to see the link between Marc Millar, the founder of the Blue Balls, and the logo, created by a friend, of the group he started. The 47-year-old photographer sports the same broad beard that, along with a stylised pair of blue balls, lunges out of the image, which can be found emblazoned across various bits of group merchandise, including a hoodie and their Edinburgh Blue Balls budgie smugglers.

Like many of the groups we came across, they have both the cool merch and the inspiring social media. In an age when formal membership of groups and communities is not as strong or extensive as it used to be, groups are being forged in new ways – through Facebook and Instagram – but they still contain echoes of the old.

It's there in the badges and the hats. As one swimmer once told us, being in a swim group can be a little like being in the Brownies or the Scouts – but for adults.

MARC MILLAR
founder of the Blue Balls

I set up Edinburgh Blue Balls because I realised, heading into my late forties, that I didn't have a supportive group of friends. I was in a complicated relationship, and I relied heavily on partying, alcohol or recreational drugs as a form of support and to escape my own feelings. I didn't have anyone to talk to about my own direction and I had lost my own identity. To compensate, I started talking to people online about my mental health. It felt easier to open up to strangers.

I started to follow swim groups online and soon realised that they offered more than just a swim; they also provided a supportive space for their members. I asked some of the groups if they would be interested in setting up an Edinburgh group and was encouraged to start my own. It took another year to build up the courage to post a meet-up. The response was overwhelming.

I'd previously been to a men's mental health support group. We all sat around a table and talked about how we were feeling, but I didn't feel comfortable participating. I really wanted something more organic where my anxious brain didn't have a week to think about what I was going to say to a bunch of strangers around a table. I really wanted something more in the moment, which is where the cold water comes in. I took the plunge (excuse the pun!) and started the journey with my own swim group. The aim was to help myself and anyone else who was feeling a bit lost, or didn't feel like they fitted in. I wanted a group where men could be themselves and not have to prove anything, a community of support for men, irrespective of their background.

It's a very uplifting experience making connections with others while freezing your balls off. As soon as you put "Men's Mental Health" in front of anything nowadays, it attracts people that are maybe looking for something else, a bit of extra support, and who will also be supportive to others. It's about trying to break down that alpha male mindset, to promote men supporting men and non-toxic masculinity.

To have a group of men who do not give a monkey's about your sexuality, body shape or clothes – everyone is there for good company, support and a kick-start to their day – is a huge deal to all of us. It feels good to have met a tribe of guys who all feel the same and share the same values. I can be myself around them, showing weakness, and that gives me strength.

The group is growing all the time. There are few places where men can get support – especially from other men. Starting up the Edinburgh Blue Balls is among my proudest moments and I have met some amazing, supportive, strong and vulnerable men who I can call up anytime for support and I hope that anyone who joins feels the same.

When we met Marc over coffee, he described how the group was inspired when he started following the Instagram account of Ice Guys North East, who swim from Roker Beach, Sunderland. When he asked if they were thinking of setting up anything like it in Edinburgh, they replied encouraging him to set up his own group. "I had," he recalled, "a couple of bottles of wine one night and did it. Before I knew it, ten people were coming the next day."

The group snowballed from there. "It's a bunch of guys," Marc said, "with absolutely nothing in common, all different ages, walks of life. Before a swim, everyone's polite. But then you dip your balls in the water and you've got everything in common, everything. You feel so much empathy."

As well as three swims a week, they also run two Facebook chat groups, one where people can go and check in if they want a bit of support, and another for organising dips.

HONEST CONVERSATIONS

What's clear, from speaking to many other swimmers, is that Marc's willingness to express his anxieties is part of his group's success. He is not only leading them into the water, but into a particular way of talking about themselves.

As Johnny Panchaud put it, "He got everyone's trust so quickly and I think that came through him being extremely transparent. For the first month he was saying, 'Guys I'm s**tting myself, I'm still terrified before every single group.' The leader of the group showing vulnerability has encouraged us to show vulnerability."

Also in attendance at some of those early swim check-ins at Edinburgh Blue Balls was John McMillan.

"As we went round," he told us, over a Zoom call, "everyone was sharing their fears and anxieties and you could see that, as it progressed, people's chests were growing bigger, almost gaining strength from the group itself."

John had found the group at a time of need, spotting it on Facebook in the run-up to the fifth anniversary of the day he tried to take his own life.

"Because I knew the anniversary was approaching," he said, "things were building up. I knew either I was going to have a total breakdown, or I needed to do something. Coming across this group was a huge weight off my shoulders. I was able to not bottle it up as much."

What John got from those early check-ins and swims spread to the rest of his life. "I've been more honest with how I've been feeling. I've been having more honest conversations with friends and family."

John stressed that he could share his problems with fellow rugby players, but that this group was something more open again. He is keen to raise awareness around mental health in all areas of his life, including his rugby. "I help coach under-14s and under-16s and, as club captain and as a coach, I want to strive to be a good role model for people and for people to know that you're going to have struggles."

WHERE TO FIND HELP

If you are feeling overwhelmed, depressed, in crisis or having suicidal thoughts, you can contact the Samaritans, who are there to listen to you, any time, day or night, on 116123. There is also, specifically for young people under 35, Papyrus UK, which provides a hotline on 0800 068 4141.

DAVID NIMMONS

Edinburgh Blue Balls

It was my partner who noticed the Blue Balls on Facebook and she sent me a screenshot. I joined the group and then I stayed quiet for a little bit, before deciding I was going to go for it.

I didn't know anyone in Edinburgh, as I'd just moved, so it was a chance to meet people.

It was this whole thing about men supporting men and mental health that appealed to me. I'd done a bit of swimming before that, up a Munro or in a waterfall somewhere, but never regularly and never with the intention of going specifically to go for a swim.

By joining the group, it was more about, how do I protect my own mental health and what can I put in place to help that?

In the past few years, I've had a lot of life challenges. My marriage ended; I struggled over my own part in that, and I've also been processing the part my ex-wife played in it . . . trying to make sense of everything. I no longer lived with my kids, didn't see them every day and that was hard, really hard. On top of that, my brother attempted suicide and that affected me deeply.

I went to my doctor and spoke to him about how I was feeling. I told him that I'd had suicidal thoughts but never to the point that I was close enough to go through with – but it was there.

I'd never been suicidal before, but I'd had self-doubt, self-loathing. I had all these thoughts about how I was not good enough – as a dad, as a husband – but never to the point of it would just be better if the car left the road on the way home. It had never got to that point. And when it got to that point, I knew I had to go and speak to the doctor, who quite quickly got me an appointment to see a talking therapist.

I started speaking to a talking therapist through the NHS, which helped massively, but I needed something else. I needed something to help me control it on my own terms.

I think part of my attraction to the Blue Balls came from what my brother did. He attempted suicide by jumping off rocks into a river and for him it was, "This cold water is going to take it away and I won't have to fight anymore, that will be it over." But for me the water gives me strength. I never leave the water feeling worse than when I went in. No matter how bad a day I've had at work, no matter how awkward things have been with my ex, or not seeing my son and daughter – once I'm in the water with the guys it's like life is beautiful.

I wanted to turn the water from something that takes everything away to something that really adds to my life.

I've never been part of a group like this – the only thing that comes close is being in the football dressing room. You've got that camaraderie, you've got that banter, but there you don't have that vulnerability and openness and honesty that the guys have got in this group. I've now got a safe space to be able to share my worries, struggles and vulnerabilities. A diverse group of friends who are always there for each other but may never have met if not for Marc and the Edinburgh Blue Balls and our collective love of the water.

MEETING OF BLUE MINDS

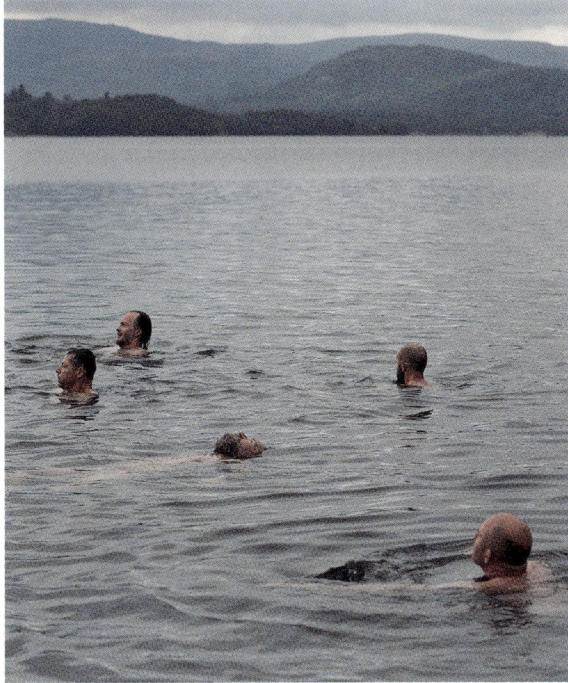

The Edinburgh Blue Balls group is not alone – and it has gone on to inspire others. In January of 2022 we met Lake District swimmers Jonathan Cowie and Gilly McArthur as they joined the Blue Balls for a dip on Portobello beach. The pair had been doing a January challenge in which they swam every day in the outdoors with different men in a bid to promote cold water swimming as good for mental health.

They were buzzing as they emerged from the water – and it was clear to us that a movement was growing.

Eight months later, Anna and I were meeting them again at Lake Windermere, where the Blue Mind Men, set up by Jonathan, were taking a dip off an idyllic wooden jetty. In an echo of that early Blue Balls gathering, they began the meeting with a circle. Names were shared, smiles and hugs, then a wade into the lake, followed by each of them, one by one, charging down the boards to throw themselves into the chill water.

"It's important to me," said Jonathan, "that everyone introduces themselves

"There is absolutely nothing else that compares to sharing the experience of a cold water swim. The mental battle to commit and go in is real, but every week the water doesn't fail to put a smile on our faces and generate those moments of camaraderie that last well beyond the experience."

Chris Cowman, Taking the Plunge, Surrey

and says their name. And then we have a bit of a check-in, and we try to keep it quite positive. It might be something that you're grateful for that week – or something you're proud of. That sets the intention that this isn't going to be a sporting endeavour. It's setting that definite intention that this is around mental health, giving people that space to share if they want to.

Several influences, Jonathan recalled, shaped the Blue Mind Men. One was his appreciation of the very strong community he found when he used to swim at Tooting Bec – and the fact that after their races there was always tea and cake, and a lot of chat. Another was his time as a member of

London Frontrunners, an inclusive LGBT+ and gay-friendly running and triathlon club, whose welcome routine at the start of a run was that everyone would stand in a circle and share just their name.

"I really wanted," he said, "that everyone would share their name – it helps people get to know each other."

What's striking in these groups is how many men talk about now having therapy alongside their swimming routine. The pandemic, Jonathan observed, had made it more acceptable for everyone to talk about their mental health. "That's something that has definitely come out of Blue Mind Men. We do talk about our mental health."

IAN WOOD
member of the Blue Mind Men

I've lived in the Lakes all my life, but I had always disliked being in the water. I had not wanted not to like it, and loved being on it, just not in it. But I was hanging out at Bobbi's coffee shop in Kendal, where we met Johnny and Gilly, and they were talking about this men's mental health swim and that it was on 31 January this year, 2023.

I just thought, you know what, let's give it a go. You're being taught by professionals how to get into cold water safely, it's the perfect opportunity.

On the day, I went down and it was absolutely ridiculous. It was −3 degrees air temperature, albeit a stunningly beautiful morning and just a smidge below 5 degrees in the water, so quite bity. I didn't go fully in that day, but we learned how to breathe, and I thought, "Okay, I can see these guys know what they're talking about." And the next morning I went and bought a dryrobe.

I came back down here, and the day was totally different. On 31 January it had been flat calm, beautiful weather . . . the next day it wasn't. There were waves. But I thought, "I'm going to do this, I'm going to get my shoulders under" – and some of the Lake Swimming Ladies were here, and they said, "Oh man, this was your first time yesterday? We'll wait and make sure you're okay."

I thought, this is the nicest community I've ever experienced – and that was it! I was in virtually every day after that. I stopped drinking. I was a heavy drinker for thirty years. Grey area drinking, I think the term is. I nearly lost my sight a couple of years ago because of blood pressure and alcohol and stuff going on, and I thought it was time for a new version of me – those guys, maybe they helped save me.

The Blue Mind Men are a great bunch of guys, there's no competition and there's no egos.

I don't think you can get that adrenaline buzz from many other experiences. One that consistently and quite quickly keeps you on that high.

Jonathan had struggled in his first winter in the Lake District – the darkness was more than he had reckoned for. He was also clear that, while being about mental health, that the group is about joy and positivity.

"I think humour is always important – so I think that coming to the water with a sense that what we're doing is really stupid is always good. It's a good way to bond with people. Even though it is about mental health, we want to make it a positive experience. Cold water swimming is a stupid thing to do. And that's one of the reasons why it's so good."

Over the months, the Blue Mind Men have accompanied many men into the water for the first time – and Jonathan has seen how bonding that experience can be. "There is that real sense of community but also a sense of support and achievement for that person – like a shared achievement that we are all doing this together. You don't get that when you're swimming on your own."

HEARTS ON SLEEVES

The way these men share their stories is testimony to something shifting, something breaking down in terms of stigma. In the UK, suicide is the biggest cause of

death in men under the age of fifty and around three quarters of deaths from suicides each year are men. In one poll, by the Priory, 77 percent of men said they had suffered with common mental health symptoms like anxiety, stress or depression and 40 percent of men said they had never spoken to anyone about their mental health.

But here we have men talking about issues they previously struggled to raise. They are reassessing their lives and needs, including the pressures on them, in a different way.

And many of them were now coming to this in midlife. One of the Blue Balls, in Edinburgh, for instance, Ryan Malone, told us, "Lockdown hit me pretty badly. But this has always been underlying. I'm forty-three. I've been speaking to a few people about why men in that age bracket are in such a bad state of mental health. For me, it was a buildup of anxiety and depression. It built up to one Sunday in

August, when my wife was in London and I was on my own. I couldn't breathe. I'd had anxiety and minor panic attacks before but with this I realised I needed to seek help. I went to the GP that Monday."

What stands out here was how Ryan talked of a midlife crisis – and that more and more men are doing so.

The midlife crisis was also something we broached when we talked to Mental Health Swims coach, Salim Ahmed. The founder of SwimLab, Salim teaches swimming as a performance art, rather than a competitive skill, and this is significant when we begin to talk about the pressures on men.

"Though the by-products," he said, "are inevitably speed and endurance through efficiency, that is never billed as the start point. To this end, I often ask most swimmers to remove watches from my sessions for the first two weeks. It's not about trying to win, but more to actually live."

Men are, he observed, becoming more aware that there are several stages to this "midlife crisis". He continued, "There's the accelerated way in which your body starts to fail, which means having to let go of your personal best and learning that you need to accept certain things are happening with your physiology.

"Men are becoming aware of that. They're starting to discover that having a swim every couple of days is making them feel so much better. And then they find that they're getting their mojo back. But they have to embrace the fact that they have to approach swimming in a different way. Not to win, but to live."

"We've now accompanied many men going into the water for the first time. When we're in a group there is that real sense of community and also achievement for that person – like a shared group achievement that we are all doing this together. You don't get that when you're swimming on your own."

Jonathan Cowie, Blue Mind Men

TOM MASON

**Blue Balls Cornwall,
@blueballscornwall**

I set up Blue Balls Cornwall with a friend two years ago. I'd started cold water swimming myself and found it an absolute game changer for my mental health. A friend of mine, who is the co-founder of a men's mental health charity called Man Down Cornwall, saw me going swimming and came along with me. Very quickly we realised that actually the benefits we were feeling needed to be shared. We wanted more guys to get in the water.

So, we set Blue Balls Cornwall up; its growth has been totally organic, and it has become much more than a cold water swimming group. It's a community now, a place where guys can connect in a non-judgemental environment. We aim to reduce the stigma around mental health and encourage each other to share all the stuff that's going on in life; it's very similar to Man Down.

We have heard some inspiring stories, including guys who use cold water to help them recover from their grief or from bad injuries, like one guy who was run down by a lorry on his motorbike and has some horrific scarring on his legs, and who uses the cold water to help his recovery process.

It really is all about the fellows who show up and challenge themselves to get in that cold water. Everyone has that initial resistance to the cold, but once you get in there is a real sense of achievement, which sets you up for the day.

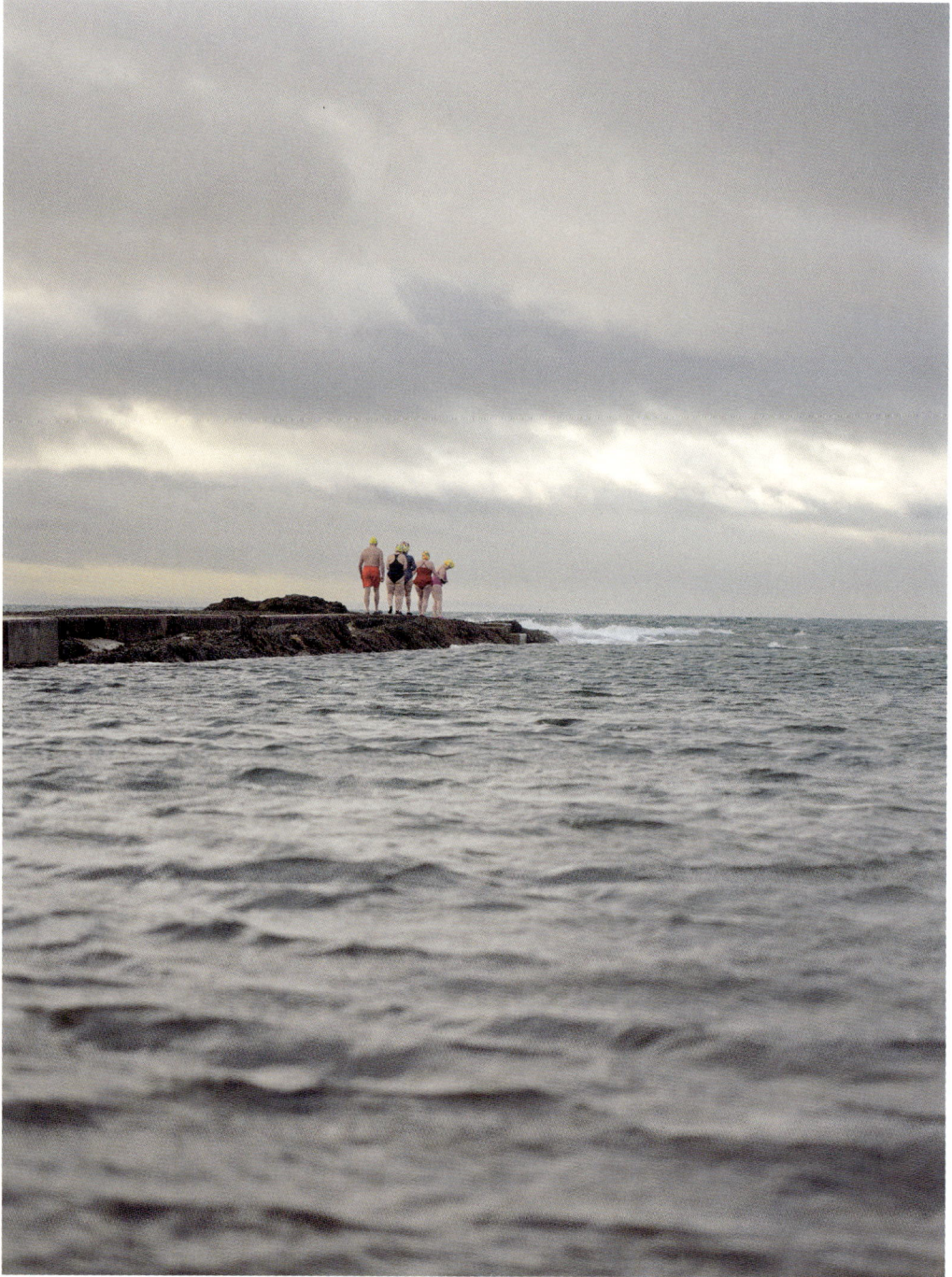

CHAPTER 3

THE
MENOPAUSAL
MERMAIDS

~~~ ~~~ ~~~

THE SWIM SISTERHOOD

The Pittenweem Menopausal Mermaids are not all menopausal, or even women in midlife, in spite of the name that many of them have embroidered on their dryrobes. They also include one 75-year-old man, a 27-year-old woman and, unofficially, a number of the mermaids' dogs.

Nevertheless, they entirely live up to their name – which embodies a kind of rebellious humour and two-fingers-up to the expectations of society, particularly those around women and what you might do or be in midlife.

It's an attitude we've come to recognise in groups all over the place, and not just of women of that age. There are touches of that rebel fun in almost every swim tribe of women we found, not simply dipping together, but supporting each other through life's difficult times.

The windswept village of Pittenweem is in the East Neuk of Fife. This former fishing community has seen swimmers come and go. Just forty years ago youngsters were learning to swim in the tidal pool, tucked beyond the headland at the west end of the village. Many of the mermaids took their first strokes there. But it speaks volumes about what happened to outdoor swimming culture in the UK that, over the decades since those mermaids were girls, the pool had fallen into disrepair, and was only recently brought back to glory – and that this was partly inspired by an idea and a petition started by one of the group.

One of them, Michelle Smith, told us that as a teenager she swam in the sea from March to October. Many of their husbands worked at sea and are former fishermen turned fish merchants. "Because you've grown up around here, you have a respect for the sea, because it's dangerous. You've got a love of the water – and you feel great."

On a chill February morning, we joined the mermaids at this pool, a stretch of grey water, flanked by old stone walls.

The group immediately paraded, in bright matching swim hats, to the end, and one by one lowered themselves in. There was singing and laughter.

What's interesting about this group is how long they have known each other. There is Julie Brooks, the American, who describes herself as "the one import", but the others are locals, and tight, having gone to school together and worked for the most part together in catering for years. Their bond was strengthened through the pandemic.

Julie grew up in America and spent the summers swimming outdoors. Her father, a swimming pool manager, had all her siblings take turns as lifeguards, and she can't remember a time in her life when she couldn't swim. Even when she lived for some years in Moscow, she swam there,

"Together we swim, embrace the silence and the cold, chat and laugh, help each other get dressed if we are too cold afterwards, and huddle around the fire with a cup of tea to warm up; we are kindred spirits."

Fran Waddington, The Blue Flamingo Swimming Group, North Yorkshire

in the summer, in the clean stretch of the river upstream from the city. Though not with those Russians who cracked a hole in the ice – they, she thought then, were mad. Now, she said, an ice dip is an ambition of hers.

Not everyone totally embraced the name when one of the members, Lisa, came up with it. "There were quite a number of us who," Julie recalled, "while we liked the name, and we thought it was funny, and we thought it was cute, we maybe didn't want it to necessarily be written everywhere. We didn't want to be branded like that. It was our, like, internal name. Ashamed is definitely too strong a word. But we sort of felt like, oh, has that got negative connotations? You know, is that going to be something where people look at us differently because of that name?

Now, however, they have the name embroidered on the bottom of their dryrobes and are owning it. "I am not embarrassed," said Julie. "It's positive . . . you know, we're starting to change as a society. Being menopausal is not a stigma anymore. It's something that's accepted."

The group started in the early days of the pandemic, in August 2020, after the first lockdown. The story goes that one of the group's members, Donna Watson, had

already started swimming outdoors, and at a party she had suggested to the rest of them that they do it. The next morning, she had them all in the sea.

The group grew from there. Among them is Lynne Muir, who recalls how when Covid started she was working in homecare and going round twelve houses in a day. Sore from constantly washing her hands, and wearing PPE, the big moment of her day was when she would meet the group at the pool at 2.30 p.m. "Everything," she said, "just disappeared out your head. You forgot about everything and later you felt able to come back and deal with it all. I know a lot of people did work through it, but I was right among it all."

YOU DON'T HAVE TO BE A MERMAID

Then there is the Bob Melville; the one man. That's one thing we've noticed about these groups that seem to be about one gender, often they are more open than their name might first suggest.

Bob, who had been the group's friend and unofficial photographer, recalled his first swim with them. "They told me one day to bring my dookers along," he said. "But I said, 'No, I'm no' going in.' Still, I put my swimming costume on, and we went along to the golf course beach, and I exaggerate greatly when I say I was in for two minutes. I was in and out – but since then it's been brilliant. That particular day,

it was snowing when we went in the water. It's great for mental health."

He spoke openly about his emotional journey. "I used to suffer, and still do, from depression. But I don't take any tablets now. This is my tablets. I haven't taken any for three years now, since swimming. Only a few weeks ago I went along, and I spoke to two of the girls and I was weepy and, by the time I came out, I was a different person altogether."

The other thing we love about these menopausal mermaids is that they do all the quirky things that swimming groups do – and we mean all – the picnics, the fancy dress, the themed trips, the skinny dips, the fundraisers, the solstice swims. And they do it big.

Over breakfast, in the Clock Tower café, run by members Laura and Lisa Hughes, they told us about their adventures. The time they had a picnic on the beach when it snowed; the full cooked breakfast eaten down at the harbour, brought there in casserole dishes wrapped in towels; the six-foot blow-up balls they tossed about the tidal pool; the swim trip to Silver Sands beach where they all wore silver; mermaids on tour; the trip where they got the boat from Anstruther to North Berwick.

"We were in North Berwick all day dressed like pirates!" said Julie. "We brought rum punch. And people were taking our pictures."

Some of the women called the group "the best thing" they had done in their whole lives. They also agreed that the group helped them in difficult times. "For me," said Julie, "there have been times when I felt low. Being in the group pulls you right up. Doesn't matter what's going on – the minute you're with the group, everything else fades. I think the other thing that's happened for a lot of us is we've given up worrying about our bodies and what we look like. It doesn't matter."

"It's not so much the swimming," said Fiona McGregor, "it's the whole thing. I live on my own. I've seen me sitting just so miserable and the minute you go, it could be a freezing cold wintery day, but the minute everybody gets together, or even a few of you get together, that keeps you going for a good few days. Yes, you get the adrenaline rush when you go in that freezing cold water, but the getting together afterwards is huge."

WONDERFUL AND WILD

The craze for middle-aged women wild swimming seems to have almost directly coincided with a strong movement urging openness about the menopause.

That perhaps shouldn't be surprising. The world of swimming reflects the wider world and what I often see among these tribes is an expression of some of the other shifts there are around mental health and busting stigma and petitioning for inclusiveness. We see groups of women supporting each other for all sorts of reasons – though, most of all, for joy.

Often what women are looking for is not just support and sisterhood, but a little bit of adventure – a chance to explore and do something with others in the outdoors. That is what is at the heart of Sarah Gerrish's Wonderful Wild Women group in the Lake District.

The skies were dark when we arrived at a car park not far from Rydal Water on a September morning. Rain trickled down our windscreens. But gradually the cars turned up, and soon a group of ten women had gathered to walk to the lake.

This, we could tell, was a hardcore group, one that would turn out in all weathers and wasn't going to be put off by the minor issue of a small downpour. Hiding under a tree, we twisted and contorted ourselves as we stripped off to wade in, rain puddling on our bags and robes.

Out on the water, I found myself chatting with Thao Nunns, as we paddled past reeds and through drizzle. Thao told me that she had come to the UK from Vietnam and had had a fear of water since she was a child. Whenever she enters the water, she said, her heart beats fast and she has butterflies.

"I had a bad accident when I was about seven or eight years old," she recalled. "I fell into a pond behind my house. My sister rescued me, but I had a memory blank. All I can remember was sitting at the bottom of the pond looking up at the white bubbles floating up. I do not remember how I got out or what happened after that."

When she met her husband, he taught her to swim in a pool, but when they came to the Lake District, living in Bowness next to the lake, she still found that water "dark and frightening".

There was a lot of talk out there on the lake, and still more as we got dressed and walked back to our cars, about the struggles of different life stages – and Sarah observed that it was easier to talk outdoors. "You feel a little bit more liberated and less self-conscious. It's a shared experience and it's nice to be with people.

It gives that regular check-in – it can be a nice start to the day – and then we're exchanging messages throughout the day."

Sarah had been studying to be an architect, and juggling that with family and a job, when she first dreamed up the group. She had been aware how important being outside and active was for her in terms of happiness and wellbeing, but she felt she didn't have anyone she could call to take to the hills with whenever she needed. Around that time, she also set up an account on Instagram which began by simply sharing women's pictures of outdoor adventure. People loved them.

Six months later, she organised her first group meet – a hike up Blencathra – then soon swimming was introduced as an element, after Sarah, who then did triathlon, saw women swimming in skins, and thought she would give it a try.

The swimming, and the group, have been a help to Sarah during her own difficult time. In 2021 she had to have an ovary removed because of a cyst. It was her only remaining ovary as, when she was just fifteen, the other had been removed owing to a tumour.

"I found that swimming was great for managing the pain prior to having the surgery," she told us. "I first got symptoms just before the pandemic, in October 2019, but I was told the cyst would probably go away, so I simply cracked on. Then I started getting pain and then it became more consistent and regular. From February

2021 right through to July, swimming was the only thing that really helped with that. It was a great tool to access for pain relief when it was needed."

She is now in surgical menopause, but recently discovered she was likely perimenopausal ever since when, at fifteen, she had that first ovary removed, though she nevertheless managed to have a family.

Wonderful Wild Women has been a support system for her in recent times. "It was," she said, "having other women to talk with. One thing I love about the community is that there are so many different ages there, and people who have experienced such different lives."

Sometimes she would come across women at the lakeside with HRT patches stuck to their bums and found it easy to open up a conversation. "They would tell you what they were going through and what research they had done themselves. All these different experiences. I was actually quite shocked. But it was a real help because that way you realise you're not on your own."

Now on a tailored new dose of HRT, including testosterone, Sarah is starting to feel better. "Sometimes just saying it out loud helps take some of the weight off. Or a good crying session by the water."

Thao Nunns, too, talked about how the cold water, and Wild Swimming Women, were, for her, a help in dealing with pain, and how it was endometriosis that eventually took her to the lake that she found so dark and frightening.

She had been suffering with pain for years, with little sympathy from her male doctor, who simply told her that her pain threshold was low and to take Paracetamol. But her friends told her to try the cold water, they assured her that it would help with pain relief.

Her husband took her for the first time to Moss Eccles Tarn on a sunny day in March. "I was so nervous entering the water," she recalled, "but my husband and the kids were there to cheer me on.

"At first," she said, "I thought it's going to be freezing and I'm going to die of shock, but it's one of the best feelings ever. I felt the cold tingling through my body up to my shoulders as I entered the water, my heart racing like mad, and when I got out my skin felt burning warm, not cold at all; it's a most refreshing feeling and the important bit is that I am alive, not as scared as I thought."

From then on, she was, she said, "addicted to the cold water". "Each time I entered for longer and could swim further with my friends. Also, every time I'm in pain, I get into the lake. It has helped me massively to control the pain and I felt great for hours afterwards."

THE RISE OF THE BLUETITS

Perhaps the most famous group centred mostly on women is the Bluetits – though in fact it declares itself to be for "everyone . . . no matter your gender, ethnicity, size, age". Now nine years old, and with groups dotted across the UK and beyond, it began as a small group of friends meeting on a beach in Pembrokeshire in 2014 and just kept growing – until in 2020 its founder decided to turn it into a social enterprise.

And the woman behind the tits is Sian Richardson. When we spoke to Sian, she was on the farm she lives at in Pembrokeshire preparing to head off to Slovenia to swim relay with the Bluetits at the ice swimming World Championships, where she was due to swim twenty-five metres in water below five degrees.

"It's gone from me," she said, "standing on my own on the shore of Lake Windermere wondering what on earth I was doing, to forty of us going as a team."

She reflected on how, at the very start of her ice swimming journey, she had gone to an event run by the same organiser, and been "very, very scared".

"I had no idea what to expect. This was my first entrance into the cold water swimming community, and it was incredible. It was, after years of doing many other sports and never particularly feeling as if I was part of anything, a moment where I thought, 'This is it.' This is definitely my group of people."

She had, she said, always liked a challenge that she considered to be "way beyond" her capabilities. Before immersing herself in outdoor swimming she had taken up running, as a means to help her through depression. "The word depression to me was horrific. I'd been brought up in a lovely, very stiff-upper-lip, get-on-with-it family. So, I was like, 'This can't be me.' I did everything that I was told to do by the doctor. I took the pills, and I hated them. I've never been a pill taker. I hated the whole thing. But the pills worked and at least got me out of that fug initially. And then I started thinking there's got to be something else here. So, somebody said you should take up running."

After doing 5km, she did a marathon, then an ultramarathon, and ultimately got seduced into triathlon, even though she had never done "head-down swimming". But something wasn't quite working for her. The problem was she never, in all these endurance sports, felt quite like part of the community.

"I always felt like I was a fraud. I was an impostor, because I used to laugh a lot and I wore very colourful clothing. But also

because I never minded being last. I never minded not finishing. I always used to think they should pay me to be there because people used to say sometimes, 'Do you mind if I cross the line before you?' I'd say, 'I don't mind at all.' I was providing a service."

Then she hit a phase when "everything started to fall apart". "I couldn't walk very well. I couldn't work out why and I knew I needed two new hips, and I would have to give up the long-distance running stuff because I was in a lot of pain." Someone

suggested that since she liked a challenge, she should try an ice mile instead.

"I didn't hear," Sian said, "the word 'ice'. I only heard the word 'mile', and I thought, well, that will be easy. Again, this was an incredible journey that took me three years to be brave enough to do. My body had to acclimatise but actually it was my brain that took a lot longer than my body."

A year later, she completed her first ice swimming event, swimming just thirty metres. She told us, "It was nothing like I'd ever experienced. It was like a warm hug. Nobody was asking me how far I could swim. Or, what was my time? They asked me how long I had been swimming and I'd say a year in the winter. And then I got the 'Wow, well done for being here ...'"

The feeling of warmth and encouragement, as well as the cold thrill, was so great that Sian went on and did another and another and another. "It was this whole thing about this community, and I've never found that to be faltering in any way. Everybody is looking out for you. People aren't judging you. People don't care about the size that you are or how fast you are particularly. It's all about this joy of getting in the water. Everybody appreciates everybody else's bravery."

THE GREAT TIT WEEKEND

A spirit of fun permeates the Bluetits, almost wherever you find them. Sian tells a story about how, the year before lockdown, she organised what she calls the Great Tit Weekend, a swim gathering at a bunkhouse on the farm campsite, of 105 Bluetits. "That was the first time we'd seen over a hundred Bluetits in one place. And what we noticed was the laughter, the community, the bonding, the way that people were completely inappropriate."

The weather, however, went against them, and they had to change their swimming plans. "The first night," she recalled, "we had a pond swim. I told them all no

"We meet early every weekday morning come rain or shine through the seasons. I moved here and felt lonely, I don't mind admitting it, but through a chance conversation I am now part of a brilliant (mad!) group of women. My life changed. A shared connection to the sea, sometimes the river and sometimes the harbour, depending on tides. We support each other through good and bad times and what is said in the waves stays there."

Tracy Acock, Bluetits, Newquay

drinking; if anybody's been drinking, nobody goes to that pond. Every fecker was drinking."

"On the Sunday, we took them to the blue lagoon, which is a National Trust old sea quarry, and I was on car-parking duty. When I started to walk over, a member of the public was on his way back and he said, 'Be careful, there's a hundred naked women in there.' I came across the top of this cliff and looked down, and I kid you not, it wasn't a hundred, but most of them naked, and they were howling like banshees. I looked at it and I thought, 'Oh my goodness me, this is amazing.'"

There are, at the time of writing, around 100,000 Bluetits, and counting, and the movement is now supported by a social enterprise which not only creates the badges, but also has provided funding for coaches, and is even behind a course in Wales that brings coaching, including water safety, to people who might not otherwise consider it, including, for instance, farming communities.

The groups, said Sian, often tend to have a particular character. "Ninety-eight percent of them," she said, "are the same. I think that's because not everyone would join a group called the Bluetits. There must be something in your brain that finds the Bluetits amusing. So, there's a similar atmosphere. They are absolutely bonkers every single one of them, but in the most delightful way."

CHAPTER 4

MENTAL HEALTH SWIMS

COMING TOGETHER FOR WELLBEING

There's a story often told – you've probably heard it yourself – about how wild swimming is good for your mental health, and that this is down to a physiological combination of cold-water shock and the dive reflex. Whenever we hear that we tend to think, yes, that's true, but is it really all of it?

Is there something missing in this explanation? Could it be, as Dr Rangan Chatterjee told us, something to do with the community, the support, the sharing and bonding?

Of course, some groups are purely social and focused on fun, but others are explicitly about support, and delivering that support to people who might not otherwise find their way to the water.

We joined one such group, run by Dr Bell's, a community centre supporting families in Leith, Edinburgh, at the beach on a bright January morning. There, on the sands, we found not only smiles and laughter, but dryrobes, neoprene gloves and boots, matching bobble hats, all provided by the centre for those who can't afford them, as well as a warming fire and hot drinks.

This was a swim session specifically designed for struggling parents with children under five years old. As we settled round the fire for post-swim chat, there was plenty of letting off steam, sharing of tales about boyfriends, Tinder dates, plans to try for a baby, the irritations of single-parent life-juggling, from a huddle of women who were warm, welcoming, upfront – and very, very funny.

There was Michelle Martins, for instance, ebullient, even as she arrived to the water. "They call me Late Michelle," she said, laughing, "because I'm always late. I'm always busy and rushing around, juggling daily life, but then I get in that water, and it completely clears your mind. You're not thinking about all the jobs that you've got to do. You're not thinking about what problems you've got. You just go in there. Having the community where we can chat and be open is so important. We say things to each other sometimes that we don't even say to our close friends. Just being in this environment is a reset button."

Then there was Christine Gilmore, who recalled her first session, a year previously, midway through a pandemic in which she had found herself stuck in the house, home-working and with tiny children, including a one-year-old – and was blown away by being out and in nature. Quickly it became a high point in the week. "I think as mothers we often don't give ourselves the time that we need to look after ourselves." The whole experience – the fire, the sea, the warm drink, the company, the

> *"The pressure is often on how to live the perfect life, be the perfect mum, be everything . . . but no, you just get to be here, in the water, connect back to nature again, and it makes a massive difference to your mental wellbeing."*
>
> **Michelle Martins, Dr Bell's**

MEGAN'S STORY

My little girl was born eight days before we went into the first lockdown – and she was my first baby, so I was a new mum. My mum and dad saw her for the first week and then weren't able to hold her again until she was three months. Honestly, looking back, I don't know how I got through it. There were times when I was standing in my mum's driveway with my newborn crying, thinking, "I don't know how to do this." But we got there. We got through it, and it was better than what I expected it to be, but coming back to work was difficult. It felt like it was so different. It was a complete shock to the system.

Danielle had been trying to get me to do it since she first started swimming in January and I was like, "Absolutely not. I hate being cold." Eventually, in April, she persuaded me, and I tried it once and that was me hooked. We started off doing swims after work occasionally – and then soon parents were finding out and asking about it and we started saying, "Why don't we do a group for it out of Dr Bell's?"

We did a pilot with the University of Edinburgh in May and started the group in August 2021. We never could have imagined what it's turned out to be, and we were very lucky in that the first group who came along were so up for it. The group we had was just phenomenal for supporting each other and being open and sharing. We didn't have to prompt that very much – they just were.

We were the facilitators, there with the equipment. It was their group. And, as much as it's for them, we really do get so much out of it. For me, with a baby, knowing that all their children were a bit older than mine meant that I could go to them for advice for myself. So, as much as we were doing it for them, it was for us as well.

There are times we have taken a break, over the summer holidays, and what we noticed when we returned after the summer break was how much our parents were missing it. I think that the first day back everybody cried. Everybody had a breakdown. That was probably the first time we realised how much it means to them. We decided not to take that big a break again.

The continuity is something we wanted to offer. Because when you are dealing with mental health it's not fixed overnight.

From my perspective, going through lockdown as a new mum, I totally felt like I'd lost my identity altogether. I felt stuck with this baby 24/7, so for me being able to be yourself at some point through the week was important. That's why we specifically said that children were not allowed to come along to the swims.

surrounding nature – she said would bring her back to something "a bit more primal".

"It grounds you," she said, "in being that human version of yourself and not just being controlled by the context that's around you. It gives you a bit of space to explore those parts of you that you maybe don't give time to. I've been coming to this group since January and it's made a huge difference, because you come to see it as a point in your week where you can take stock, reset. It puts you in a better place to keep going with things. I've been in various groups, and I think for me this is the most important one, because it connects you with these elemental bits of yourself that you forget about."

Mental health is important across society, but the mental health of parents, particularly lone mothers, is key not just for

the parents themselves, but for the young lives that depend on them.

As Megan Henry, one of the facilitators put it, the group is "about women looking after themselves". She said, "If you're not well, how can you look after your children? It's taking that time out, which people very rarely do. Most of the women had never left their children anywhere. But, with this, they could leave them in our creche."

The group was formed by Megan, along with Danielle Campbell, friends and colleagues at Dr Bell's, after they had come to cold water swimming as a way of coping with their own challenges during the Covid pandemic.

For Megan, the struggle had been being a first-time mum with a baby (see Megan's Story on page 86), born eight days before the start of the first lockdown. For Danielle, it was being on her own through lockdown and the first year of the pandemic. Her dog had been diagnosed with cancer in the first lockdown and she had been unable to see friends and family, with whom she was very close.

"I couldn't go to my mum's, and I couldn't go to the vet," Danielle recalled. "At one point, I felt I don't want to be here anymore. I'm on my own. Everybody else has got someone else, but I haven't. My mum and dad live five minutes away and I used to see them all the time, so I struggled with that. By the second lockdown I

went through this full breakdown and felt suicidal."

Both women still share their emotions, even now, with the group. "I cried today," said Danielle. "It was something about being in the water together. That's like a ripple effect. One person starts crying and then we start crying and then suddenly we're all hugging. We're in a huddle, hugging."

What's striking is that this is not a group of women who would have otherwise found swimming an accessible activity. "When we first spoke about it, some of the parents were saying, I can't do that," said Danielle. "I don't have a dryrobe and it's all these yummy mummies with loads of money that do it. And we were like, *Hello.* Look at us. It was taking the barrier away to say, we can give you the stuff. And even in the summer when the group wasn't running, we were letting them borrow the kit."

And, they say, the evidence is there that it is making a difference. The women do questionnaires about their mental health at the beginning and end of each term. On the group's last term, there was one parent who scored herself a one, the lowest score, and by the end of the term, she scored herself an eight.

"I think," said Megan, "it's so important, especially for the long-term parents, because we're seeing such highs and lows. We've been doing this for over a year now and so we've had a few women for that period of time, and I think it's about having that community to come and talk to. It's having that space to come and talk that is totally honest and open and that you won't get judgement from. Above anything else, that's the most important thing."

There's a ripple effect in motion here, too. Other people have already been inspired to set up similar groups in Edinburgh – for instance, one for women who are experiencing homelessness. They see what Megan and Danielle have done and how that can be replicated and adapted to other groups, other parts of the community who might not otherwise come down to the water.

THE OPEN INVITATION OF MENTAL HEALTH SWIMS

One of the people who has done the most to drive a movement around mental health and swimming is Rachel Ashe, founder of the peer support community Mental Health Swims.

"I don't think it's the cure, by the way," Rachel said over a video chat. "That's something I always try and say; I think it's really important. I don't like the idea that swimming is the answer to everything, because I just don't believe that."

Rachel, who did her first swim on New Year's Day 2019, then quickly went on to set up a monthly swim at her local beach (the precursor of Mental Health Swims), describes herself as "living with mental illness". "I'm probably," she said, "what you would call recovered now. I live a very full, happy life alongside my mental illness. Obviously, I have ups and downs, bad days, but, on the whole, life's pretty good now. I think that's partly because of swimming. But it's not such a desperate need anymore."

Mental Health Swims, she noted, is not about having to join a talking therapy

RACHEL'S SWIM MUSINGS

It's the cold on your feet, as you're walking in, the cold as it hits your private parts, and then you're having a pee and telling other swimmers that's what you're doing. In what other situation are you able to say to people "I'm peeing" in front of them and that is socially acceptable? The kind of conversations you have are a bit like the ones you would have in a toilet on a night out, when you're under the influence. Except the influence here is the cold water.

I think the important thing about swimming is it's about doing something together, and maybe partly as well about doing it outdoors. It's also that things are too complicated these days, and doing something as basic as being human beings outside doing something together feels nice. Cooking on a little fire on the beach feels pretty good. So does going for a walk with people. All these activities feel good.

I always come back to the Moomins. I love the Moomins, and on my happiest days. I feel like I am in Moominland, and I am a little Moominmamma and it's simple. It's simple pleasures. Isn't it? Also being a lesbian, I loved the idea of Tove Jansson and Tooti (Tuulikki Pietilä) on their little island trying to build their jetty, and it keeps being washed away. It's this simplicity. I have a longing for it. I sometimes think, wouldn't it be nice to live in a little cabin in the woods?

But these are actually quite privileged pleasures, and our aim is to make it easier to join in for people who would love the idea of that and for whatever reason feel there is just too much of a barrier. With Mental Health Swims, that message that you can is very clear. You can ask questions. There's lots of reassurance. People know that the volunteers have done some mental health awareness courses.

group in the sea. "I think," she said, "the title makes people feel, 'Oh, I'm going to have to share everything about myself.' That's absolutely not it. But if you want to come along and share and know that you're going to be in a safe place, one where you will be listened to and understood, then this is it. And if you behave and act a little bit differently to other people, it's going to be okay."

The idea of going into the water to process life, she observed, isn't a new phenomenon. Humans have been doing it for millennia. We have, she said, been swimming outdoors "forever".

"I think water is an environment that helps us process things. And it's connection as well, especially when you have been through something, or maybe are continually going through something. Coming to the water and being with other people is almost like a gateway into real life."

What also made the difference was spending time with other people in the water, and in what for her felt like a safe space. "It's like if you've got a dog, there's something about walking your dog and having conversations with people while you're walking a dog. I think, when you've been unwell, that is good as a practice for getting back into the world and into society. When you've been out of it for a while, and not felt like the world is a very safe place, those little conversations are a good practice."

Time in the water, Rachel observed, can be "transformational" – and that transformation isn't only about the cold. "It's about people being people and feeling like they can be themselves. That's why it's so transformational. It's people feeling safe to be themselves and say how they're feeling, if they want to. And, also, it's being comfortable on the beach or wherever you are and feeling okay to be yourself. When you're swimming, you're even more yourself, because you're really bloody cold, and you're not wearing clothes. It's hard. It's a difficult thing. Getting into cold water is difficult, and everyone shares that difficult experience together."

She feels, however, that we should be careful about overselling the benefits, or putting emphasis on the idea that swimming might be a replacement for medication. "I don't like the whole chat around, 'You'll be able to come off your antidepressants.' Because, for a lot of us, taking medication for our mental illnesses is the thing that keeps us going. I think anything which stigmatises that is not helpful."

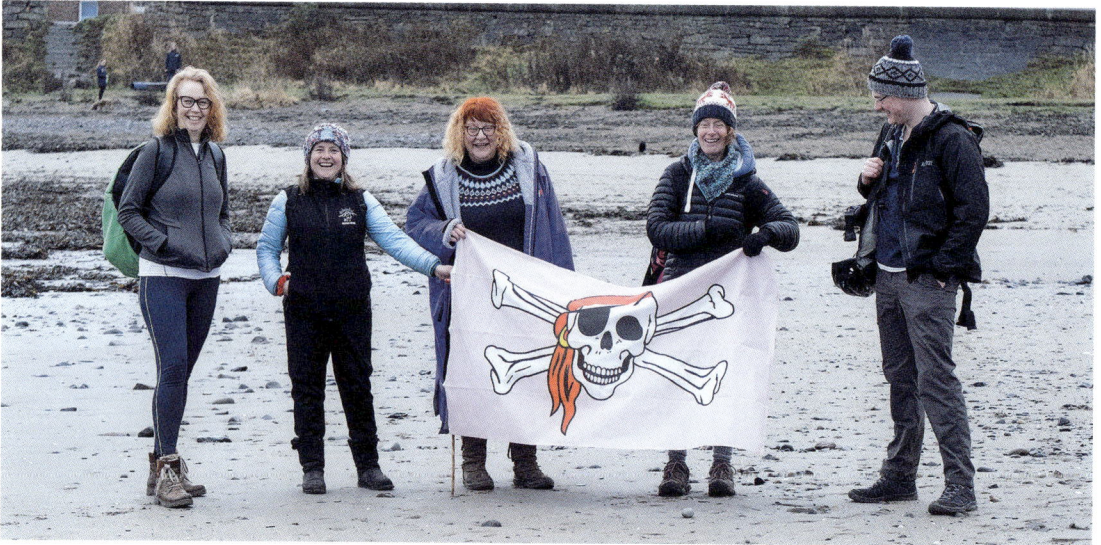

SWIMMING FOR ALL

What, above all, Mental Health Swims aims to do is create welcoming spaces that feel easy to join. The emphasis is on accessibility – and, to this end, the social enterprise is also branching out into coaching and sessions in swimming pools, with a view to inviting more people in. Swimming, after all, tends to be dominated by white, middle-class types.

"It's super white here in Wales, and I still think it's like a massive success when I see one brown face in the odd group that we have, and it is definitely changing. There are more groups where there is at least one brown face, and that feels great. But oh, my gosh, there is a long way to go.

"Our goal is always going to be access to peer support. So, for us, we are growing and moving into heated pools, so that we can have our groups in inner city locations, and also locations where at the moment

there's a lot of pollution. But we hope from those groups that people will think, I would like to give outdoor swimming a go now."

Currently Mental Health Swims have around 350 volunteers and around 150 locations. "But they're all quite small communities, because we want to keep them that way. We keep things small where possible, because that's a little bit less scary. There's always a set number of people that can sign up and it's up to the volunteer to set the number they feel comfortable with. So, some people do dinky dips, as we call them, which are just smaller groups."

But Mental Health Swims is, of course, part of a much wider movement around mental health, which expresses itself in so many different types of groups – from male mental health groups to refugee groups to student dippers. One of these is the student swim group, the Edinburgh University Bluetits, which began, like so many communities, during the pandemic.

TINKA HUGHES
student

When I was in first year, it was early pandemic, and we were stuck in our halls and that was very isolating. But one night, me and my friend suddenly said, "Let's go swimming tomorrow." We met quite early in the morning and cycled down on Just Eat bikes to Portobello.

After that amazing swim we decided to make it a weekly thing and go every Friday, in the morning. Slowly more and more people joined us. It was a nice way of meeting people. Last year, we set up an informal Facebook group and more started joining and soon we had about ninety members – but this year, 2023, I thought, why not make it an official group? And it's been such a success.

I study Sports Science and I'm interested in why cold water swimming has such an impact. I already knew when I set up the society that this was such an incredible thing for mental health. You get outside and there's the blue effect and the green effect, nature, the sky and the sea. Your endorphins are instantly released once you get out and see blue sky and greenery. And by the sea you get both.

At university you encounter so many different people with different mental health issues. Being in halls is always hard for students, whether it's Covid or not. It's always difficult to go into this place where you don't know anyone, you don't know the city very well and you are literally dropped into the deep sea and have no idea where to go. Uni can be such an isolating place if you find it difficult to socialise.

Swimming is an incredible way to feel like you're part of something. You don't need a specific skill to be able to swim in cold water. There's nothing that you need to be good at. There are lots of societies where you do need a skill – but this one is so inclusive. Everyone can go down to the beach, have a chat, have a swim, have a cup of tea after, and it's still being part of something without having that added pressure that you have to be good at it. We even have some people come along who don't swim.

It's accessible, it's not competitive, and it's nice to meet likeminded people. It's also great to do something outdoors, and without alcohol. Why should university be all about getting drunk and going to the pub, or meeting people through drinks? I didn't enjoy uni sport for that reason; I don't like getting drunk every Wednesday, nor did I like being part of this team that seemed to be there to social climb. I really miss playing sport but actually swimming, with all these people I don't know, is basically like being part of a team. Often people who play team sports come and say, "It's so nice being part a team that isn't competitive and isn't about getting drunk or about being competitive to be drunk."

It's nice being part of a team where everyone is together and wants everyone to succeed. You see that in the swimming. You see people say, "Come on, you can do it!" It's amazing, seeing that kind of team spirit.

SO GOOD, IT SHOULD BE MADE A PUBLIC HEALTH MEASURE

How much of the transformative effect of swimming is the time spent together and how much is the cold water? It's hard to tell, but research is increasingly showing that a series of cold water dips can help on multiple levels. There is even talk about it being seen as a "public health measure" or socially prescribed on the NHS.

Among those driving this shift is Mike Morris, who runs Chill Therapy, a not-for-profit that provides sea swimming courses as a form of therapy for people with anxiety and depression.

"My goal," Mike told us, "is that one day this therapy will be funded by the NHS. So, if someone comes along and says, 'I'm feeling depressed,' GPs can say, 'Do you want to take a pill or do you want an eight-week set of sessions in the sea?' It costs £100 to do those sessions. It's very cheap. It's very easy to do."

He is already creating, around the country, a network of Chill hubs – with some already in place in East Lothian, Wales, Cornwall, London, East Midlands, Kent and Dorset – so that when the NHS take it on as a treatment, people can be directed to their nearest hub.

"Our idea," he said, "is that the sea or the lake does the therapy, and we are basically allowing people to be safe in the water. We are presenting the therapy to them, and they get on and get into the water and have fun."

Mike's interest in the wonders of wild swimming was sparked when he was running an endurance event called Exmoor Open Water Swim and found that increasing numbers of participants were going into the water without a wetsuit on. At first, he thought about banning them, but then realised how much he liked their attitude. "I thought, God, how do they not die in there?" he said. "But also, I noticed that when they got out, they were always elated, and they were so on top of their game. I was gobsmacked at how they were just owning it and really exuded confidence. So, I got to talking to them. And they said, actually we do it for our mental health."

Mike was wowed by this idea and rapidly began to consider its potential as a therapy. "I thought, wouldn't it be nice to take people into the water who have anxiety, depression. That was my idea."

Mike then contacted various cold water experts. This led, eventually, to him having a meeting over tapas with Dr Mark Harper (who happens to be a key expert that Anna and I have been in contact with since early on in our swimming journey).

"My idea," said Mike, as he recalled that meeting, "right from the word go, for some unknown reason, was wouldn't it be amazing if we could find proof that actually going into the water does make you feel good. We *know* it makes you feel

> *"You get in that water and it's like a clean slate. I've come here and shared some pretty dark stuff and cried and everything like that. It's so lovely having the group of mums. We all get on, we've all shared things. We give each other support and encouragement."*
>
> **Lizzy, Dr Bell's**

good, but wouldn't it be amazing to discover the categoric truth that it does work for anxiety and depression and other sorts of illnesses."

Mike received funding to roll out the swimming sessions which he began in the first summer of the pandemic. Those attending were required to fill out forms that asked questions which ultimately indicated how depressed they were.

The team also measured inflammation levels in the blood, pre- and post-swim. This was key: Mike and Mark share a theory that people with depression have high inflammation levels. They were predicting that when people went into the water their inflammation levels would reduce.

The results, after seventy people had completed the course, showed that participants were less depressed by about 60 percent – and even after three months depression was dramatically reduced. Mike and Mark also went on to do further courses and research on whether swimming reduces burn-out among NHS staff

– and they are now doing a bigger piece of research into anxiety and depression.

Mike cited countless examples of people who believe they have already been helped. "We have anecdotal stories of people who had twenty panic attacks a day and then went down to nothing. We had people who reduced their antidepressants by half or came off them. We had someone whose brother had just died and, when they came to us, they could hardly get out of bed, but now they felt able to go back to work."

The sessions, he said, work well in tandem with mainstream treatments like CBT and anti-depressants, but are not for everyone.

It's also the case that Mike does not believe these outcomes are purely down to cold water effects. A key element, he told us, is the group. "At the end of the day it doesn't matter why it works if it does. But if one was to hypothesise, I would say a big part of this is the group therapy – combined with the intensity of the experience. If you have a group of young men who go to war and they go to hell and back, they make friendships which will last a lifetime. A lot of these people who we're dealing with have become lonely, especially with Covid, and they are not having the relationship opportunities they should have. And not only are they meeting a new group of friends with the swimming, but they are likeminded friends."

He continued, "The peer support they receive is important, as is the fact they are not doing something minor like tiddlywinks. They are getting into very cold water. They are sometimes bashed by big waves. It's pretty bloody scary. We're constantly dealing with panic attacks, which they get over; we can treat that in the water. They carry on and they are so empowered when they've done it that they're on a buzz. Yes, they're on that buzz because they're stimulating the vagus nerve, but also because they're sharing the experience with other people."

CHAPTER 5

THE
POLAR BEARS

COMMUNING IN COLD

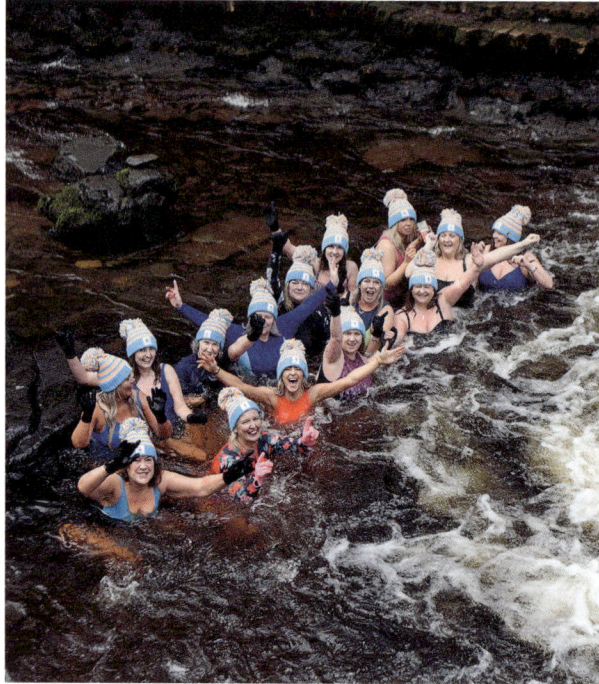

"You can't hide in the cold," said Amanda Braid. "You can't hide your pain. You can't hide your fears or your worries or your suffering or anything."

For some, the water is not about swimming. It's about cold, or cold water therapy, or even ice. It's about temperatures that dip low, towards five degrees, and beyond; the chill of a cold shower, or a glacial lake. It's Wim Hof, Susanna Søberg, Andrew Huberman and other scientists and gurus. It's coming together to crack a hole in the ice or take a dip in the winter ocean, gathering there, as some might around a warm fire.

It's what that does to you. It's where it takes you to.

These days everyone talks about the legendary Wim Hof, but we can't credit him with entirely inventing this cult of cold. That existed long before the Iceman became a household name. It must have been there back in 1525, the year to which the oldest evidence of Russians swimming in ice holes is dated. It's been there in the Russian Walrus groups that swear by the health-giving benefits of this swimming practice. It's there in the Russian tradition of dipping into cross-shaped holes, hacked into the ice, on the Epiphany – not just once, but three times in honour of the Holy Trinity and Christ's baptism in the Jordan.

Why do they do it? Mostly it's said to wash away their sins, but some believe the tradition is pagan in origin and priests have even claimed it desecrates the true meaning of the Epiphany celebration. It reaches, in other words, back to something even older than the Orthodox Church.

The idea that cold, while dangerous, does something profound to us has a deep human history. In the UK, we may not feel specifically connected to indigenous traditions, but there are now plenty of cold enthusiasts. The Polar Bears, Ice Guys North, Ice Women. The big question is what takes them there.

One of these groups is Ignite Your Fire Within, run by Martine and Amanda Braid,

charismatic sisters who have done the Wim Hof training, visited him at his centre in the Netherlands, and are now training to be instructors.

A morning spent with them, however, felt like something a little different. It had its own distinctive Braid style – and was also a reminder of how the dip often starts long before you even enter the water. At the car park, for instance.

Campsie Fells car park, a gaggle of orange and sky-blue bobble hats, all with the name Ignite Your Fire Within badged on. Silent disco headphones were clamped over our ears and the music started: *I'm on my way from misery to happiness.* Arms were immediately waving in the air. The Proclaimers cranked heads not long out of bed into life as, like some gang of joyous Minions, we raised arms in the air and began to stomp up the track. Voices were singing out loud in unison: *I'm on my way!*

Ten minutes later, clothes were being peeled off as women balanced on muddy ground, searching for dry patches on which to place kit bags. The group were on their way, a chain of bodies picking their way down over rocks to the waterside, reaching out hands and helping each other over the slippery stone and to the water's edge, where they plunged. The air vibrated. Not only with the thunder of the water, but with their squeals and the music pumping from the sound system perched on the rocks.

This was how the Braid sisters entered the water. It was how their band of women arrived at the cold, in synchrony, to the beat of togetherness, as one by one, they screamed at its bite.

It is hard to imagine a trippier start to the day.

With the Braid sisters, there is always music, dancing and laughing, and often a silent disco. "We love to dance," said Amanda. "It changes your state. No matter where you come from, it changes your emotional state. Music is powerful. Moving your body is so powerful."

"With all of our classes," Martine said, "we like to take people through a high and low state. Sometimes we start our classes with a low, a focused meditation or a mindset, and then we'll go up high with energy, with music, with movement. And then we come back down, because that's how you connect with your heart. That's how you feel that emotional state. We like to ultimately leave people feeling really high. We always end with a dance."

And, at the centre of this, is the cold. That is what all the buildup is for. At the base of the crashing waterfall, the women spread out in a line. They were breathing

"I started my journey because I had long Covid. The cold water definitely helped. The breathwork actually made me think about breathing properly. But it also had a huge impact on my mental health. I had become isolated, not really seeing people. But this meant I could come along, be part of a bigger group without being under any pressure to share things, and yet have support."

Angela, Ignite Your Fire Within

together. The water thundered like a drumroll in the background. They were like that for a while, until again, the music was turned up and one by one they took their turn to stand at the waterfall's blast – and to scream.

The buildup, the sisters believe, is an important part of the experience – as is doing it together with other people, the moment of reflection in the water, delving into your breathwork, then giving gratitude for the day. Getting out our heads and into our hearts.

"The arrival, with the music," said Amanda, "is about everyone being in sync with each other and supporting each other. One of the beautiful things that happens is that people come together and help each other into the water. They help each other out, make sure you're okay, share their hot drinks. This is all about building that community. Even if you come along alone, you don't leave alone. We're all sisters. We're all one at the end of the day."

For them, she said, that building of community is the most important thing. "You never know where anyone is emotionally when they come here, but you can guarantee that when they leave, they feel as if they're part of something bigger than what they've just gone through. It's powerful. At the end, we do a car park dance, the Hokey Cokey, or something silly; it's about releasing our inner child. As adults we sometimes forget that we can be playful, and we can be silly. Even when we've got children of our own. There's power in that. It takes you to a different place."

This particular waterfall in the Campsie Fells also has a very special place in Amanda and Martine's hearts. They began their journey in wild swimming after the death of their father, who had been a keen swimmer himself, and this was among the places where he had taken them as children.

"When we were kids, everyone else," said Martine, "went to the swimming pool and we came here with my dad. We grew up in the cold water, but as we got older and life got in the way, we stopped going. I think that's why we do love it; we can be children again. We wish we could bottle the joy we get out of the cold water and give it to people – but now we've got this community of women who are going to the water together and receiving it."

MARTINE & AMANDA

Our journey in cold water began when we lost our dad. In 2018, he was diagnosed with terminal cancer and died a very short time later. It was extremely traumatic for us to go through that with him. Had it not been for that, we wouldn't be on this journey and our lives would look very different today. It was our dad who first introduced us to wild swimming when we were young by taking us to all the outdoor places he swam in when he was a boy and telling us stories about them. When he died, it left a huge hole in our hearts, and we were lost for a very long time. Then, during lockdown, we went back out into the cold water. We felt drawn there. Instantly, we felt more alive and connected with our dad. We have gone into the cold water every day since and found ourselves beginning to heal.

We never set out to start a business, we just wanted to heal our hearts, but as the months rolled by, we realised how lucky we were because we were both on this journey together, supporting each other with our mum, and we're all close. But some people don't have that, and we wanted to help women know they are not alone in whatever struggle they are facing. Ignite Your Fire Within was born out of pain and loss and grief, and it cemented our bond as sisters. It made us closer.

When we were in our trauma, we could see so much pain around us. We don't know if it's just that when you're in pain, you see pain. Sometimes you don't notice the pain of others when you're not in that place. But when you are in that place, suddenly other people's grief is highlighted.

People started asking us what we were doing and if they could come to the water with us because they were struggling with their own lives. That's how our wellness group came about; it has been built from pain, grief, and love. And we think that's why it is such a beautiful community. It's all about love.

We wanted to learn as much as we could. We did Wim Hof training, and we went over to spend a weekend with him as well. Meeting him in person was a life-changing experience. He was a massive part of our healing, and we will always be grateful to him. We learned from Wim that the cold isn't just one thing, it is breathing and commitment (or mindset) as well. Wim aims to spread the message of love – that we can heal our bodies, we can heal ourselves. And we firmly believe that. We think his message is a powerful one. He is someone who wants to heal the world and he wants to help people. There's no hidden agenda with him. He's very true to who he is.

When you go into the water as part of a group of women, there's a connection, a sisterhood, a sense of belonging and love. That's what we feel when we're with people in the water. You see people's struggles. You see people's life stories right in front of you. You see people experiencing emotional moments, sad moments, happy moments, joyful moments. It's a whole ripple effect, because you can go to the water and still not feel great. But when you're part of something like this, in a group, the energy is so high. The joy is so high that you almost forget yourself. You're childlike. You're playful. Because you're in this experience of everyone doing it together, you don't feel alone anymore.

We believe that having a positive mindset is key to everything; it is like a tree with cold-water therapy as a huge branch of that. As well as the cold water, we are committed to lots of personal development training, such as life coaching, certified breathwork practitioner courses, holistic therapies such as reiki drumming and sound healing, as well as meditation. Combining these with the cold water every day has been transformational for us. And – through our classes, groups, and online community – our mission now is to give women the practical tools they need to step into the highest versions of themselves through love, connection, cold water and sisterhood.

STONE COLD SOBER

On our journey through cold water groups, one element that stood out was the vibrant section of the community that revolves around sobriety. For some, it's simply about rejecting drinking culture – but for many it's part of a recovery journey. It's about finding a way out of drug or alcohol addiction.

Among those is a group called Max Kolbe.

The first question when you come across this group might be who, or what, is Max Kolbe. The name, in fact, is an abbreviation of Maximilian Maria Kolbe, the patron saint of, among other things, drug addicts, who was canonised in 1982. Before it became a group, the moniker was the social media alias of Paul Donnelly, a firefighter, who was on his own journey with regards to alcohol and recovery.

Kolbe, who is renowned for volunteering to die in place of another man, whose life was thus saved, in the Auschwitz death camp, was a Conventual Franciscan friar. And for Paul, this spoke volumes. St Francis was a lover of animals and nature, and for him, that is key in his cold water experience.

"Nature opens you up," Paul said. "I found the best therapy for me was coming up here. The trees and the natural world have complete acceptance of me, even when I haven't got it myself – and that's where I learned therapy, through nature."

Max Kolbe has evolved over two years. It started with Paul talking about his own experiences and signposting to other groups and activities, then morphed into a group that did outdoor activities together. Some of these revolved around the teachings of Wim Hof, and often they still do.

But for Paul it's not entirely about the cold – though that is central to a lot of what they do. "You have to be careful about idealising the wrong things. Is it the cold? The cold is the vehicle to take you there."

There are, he said, other activities he could harness to help people in recovery. "I'm convinced I could take a group of people in recovery from drink and drugs, and I could get them into crochet, or I could take them hunting or we could focus on those rocks that kids paint. We could arrange to do it every week so they could have something to look forward to and have something to practise that would take them away from their environment that's causing them problems. That would work."

Paul continued: "That's why I think there's far too much emphasis put on the water. There are other things that are happening subtly and simultaneously in the background. But water is easily accessible in Scotland and, if you want that thrill and excitement, you can jump off rocks, you can plunge into pools. You're still getting

"I have rheumatoid arthritis. Being with the group is a big thing for me, people you feel safe with and trust. It can sometimes be quite physically challenging for me to get in the water – and they are there to help me. I can feel quite unstable on my feet when the ground is sharp. But it's worth it for that feeling in the water where it numbs all the pain."

Maryanne Jacobs, Max Kolbe

the high that people seem to be chasing."

Nowadays, Max Kolbe feels bigger than Paul – though he is still its axis, a gentle, generous figure who doesn't seem to over-manage the group, but inspires and lets it do its own thing. As we met him, and a gathering group set on walking to a waterfall, one Sunday morning in the Pentlands, he described how it wasn't now about addiction.

"A lot of the members' own stories are rooted in addiction. But not everybody's. We find that what people are looking for sometimes is a healthier relationship with alcohol. This was my vision of trying to have people from all walks of life who are all trying to do different things. No two people are using the group for the same reasons."

When we joined them that Sunday morning, it felt like dropping in on a festival event. On the walk to Flotterstone waterfalls, I fell into step with a couple wheeling their baby along in a pushchair. Gareth had been coming, he explained, since lockdown when he first heard about Paul and went sober. He was now two years sober.

"You hear a lot of people saying," he said, "Oh lockdown was so bad for me,

but lockdown was the best thing that ever happened to me. I stopped drinking. I stopped smoking cannabis. It totally changed my life. I've got the rewards for it now. I've got my wee baby boy and family."

That turnaround began when he joined Max Kolbe and immediately decided, after the first meeting, that this was the life he wanted. "I now know," he said, "that when I'm not doing the cold water swimming, I struggle a lot more. My partner is quite good at reading my character and knows when I'm needing it, so she'll encourage me. She'll push me on."

When we reached the falls, gushing with chill March water, smaller groups split off, doing their own things, and people entered the water at different times. It felt like an organic flow of activity. Overlooking the waterfall stood another small group chatting. Among them was one young woman who ran an outdoor adventure group for those who are "sober, sober-curious, or want an alternative way of living without a hangover".

"When I stopped drinking," she said, "I started off doing thirty new things in thirty days to sidetrack my mind. What I quickly realised was it was all outdoors stuff that I was falling in love with. It was all about nature."

Many will say this. They will tell you it's about the cold, and about the company, of course, but they will often also say it's about nature. Human company, cold water, nature. One former addict in recovery, Kenny Neilson, even showed us the green statue of Mother Nature, who he prayed to each morning.

PAUL DONNELLY
twelve steps to cold water

I had been sober for a while when I started Max Kolbe. I'd been using the twelve-step fellowship and other groups. But I'd started noticing, even in recovery, that sense I used to have when I used to drink, that there must be more than this.

I remember that first swim in the cold, when a friend took me to Loch Lomond. I felt, in the water, like there was something holding my whole body. I don't know how to describe it – if it was spirit, energy, whatever it was – but I felt like I was being held by something other than me. And I noticed that, for me, having lived for most of my life inside my head, I was there, and I was present, and that other thing that was there was present too.

My childhood was relatively normal – but my dad's brother was murdered, and then he lost my gran in quick succession. As a wee guy it was like I was brought up on death and, for the young, underdeveloped mind, it bamboozles the mind that things are no longer here that could be here. It probably left me with an unhealthy obsession with death, which I know now wasn't a normal childhood.

I played football and I boxed through high school, and I never had an interest in drugs and alcohol. But when the football stopped, I was working in the bank and I had the feeling, *Is this it?* I had reached working age and I'd thought the blueprint of my life was so much more than how it worked out for me.

Finding drugs and alcohol felt like "this is it". That feeling of separateness went away. I suppose with alcohol and drugs I started to feel what I now see as a unified consciousness. A lot of the drinking and drugging were social, and I was in places where there was a togetherness. I started to feel part of it all, more complete.

But that thing I needed to make me feel whole was poisoning me at the same time – and I got to the point that all the people had gone, all the sense of unity had gone, and I found myself in isolation doing all the things I was once doing for socialising.

By this point I started to experience loads of traumatic incidents with the fire service, where I worked. Basically, I was seeing other people experience shock and loss and struggle, and it had no sense of meaning to it. My whole life started to feel like virtual reality – and I started to feel like I was surrounded by death. At this point I was losing people to mental health, friends dying of cancers and illnesses. I know a lot of people go to work to escape that, but I was surrounded by it.

I thought about suicide and had all these different plans, but then my brother did make a serious attempt on his own life. When I got the news that he was in intensive care, I was catapulted into virtual reality – nothing seemed real. You're hoping it's a dream and you're certain it is happening. It's a form of denial.

But at that time the only thing I knew of to numb the pain was what I usually turned to. I felt the guilt of my brother being in intensive care while I had to turn to alcohol and drugs to have the strength to go to his bedside. I had so much guilt and shame; I was supposed to be his older sibling, I was supposed to look out for him. I knew that it had to change. That was a real turning point.

I'm now clean, I'm sober. My wee brother has had a different journey from me, but at one point he was involved in the group. It was a massive thing for my family, after all that, to see us going out and climbing hills and dipping in water.

Before I did that swim at Loch Lomond, I'd been looking for all the right stuff – connection, contentment – in all the wrong places. And this was just me getting a little sample, a little insight of what it actually feels like to be present.

Max Kolbe has taken its own shape over two years. Originally it was just me talking about my own experience in the outdoors, but it evolved. One of the first trips we did was a Ben A'an hill walk, cold exposure, and then we started doing bootcamps.

I'm still working as a firefighter. I think I'm a lot more equipped to deal with those feelings. You'll always encounter situations with distressed people. We had a fatality recently and I felt I was able to be there more for the people in that time of difficulty. That's probably true in life. My mum lost her best friend to motor neurone disease recently, and I'm in a position to be there for people today – which is so important to me. I can get caught up in the past and thinking, "You weren't then." But I am now. And I can do that in the family, and I can do that at my work.

EXTREME COLD

Max Kolbe is not the only group using cold water to help people in recovery or who are struggling with anxiety and depression. There are many others across Scotland and the UK – including the Polar Bear Club, a group started by recovered alcoholic Kenny Neilson.

What some members of the Polar Bear Club have done is quite dangerous and Kenny delivers a message of caution around extreme cold therapy. Though he started off by doing his own experiments with cold, he later began to work with Valerjan Romanovski, a Guinness World Record holder for cold endurance.

This was kicked off by the fact that one of the Polar Bears is, like Valerjan, Polish and thus knew of his superstar cold feats. "For Miro," said Kenny, "Valerjan is his superhero, perhaps the equivalent of Wim Hof if you're from Poland. This guy has seriously messed about with cold, but he's also about the safety element. He's all about what's happening in the body and what's happening in the cold."

Valerjan Romanovski has visited

Scotland and done work with the group in a cold water unit at Loch Tay, and the Polar Bears have also been out to Kraków University, in southern Poland, to be tested in his ice tanks there and competed at an international ice dipping championship in Mielno on Poland's Baltic coast.

Kenny described his own experiences: "The first time was probably the hardest thing I've ever done. After fifty-two minutes I lost the plot. My mind went and the medic asked if I was okay. I looked at him and answered in an aggressive way and they got me out. I had gone into stage two hypothermia. If I was in the real world, I wouldn't have been able to help myself. I could accept sitting in there and feeling uncomfortable. I could accept the pain. The pain was fine. It was the aftermath, the warming-up process, which was horrific, one of the most horrific processes I have been through."

He has sat in those ice tanks again since – on one occasion, in Kraków, dipping in and out of a tank at minus fifty. Then, he said, the aftermath was "another world" because he knew what to expect. What is striking is that one of the things he has learned from this experience is the importance of safety.

"Valerjan Romanovski," he said, "says there are all these groups in the world, and they are all taking people into water at zero degrees, and there's hardly any of them who understands what hypothermia is. He told us to stop doing our retreats until we understood it."

Why, we asked him, did he think so

many people in recovery were turning to cold water?

"Even though," Kenny said, "we're right into the science and work with the world's best, I always say to people, 'Forget the science.' Put yourself into the uncomfortable position. If we can fight through uncomfortable situations, then we can take that into our everyday life."

He believes it's not just about the power of the cold – though that "is undeniable" – but about people getting up in the morning, travelling to a new place, shaking the hand of someone new, doing the walk to the site – and then getting in. He also looks at it through the context of twelve-step.

"It's connecting human beings together. That's what it's all about. With twelve-step, what it tells you is, when all else fails, go and find somebody who needs a hand. Because, as soon as you go and help somebody else, you're taking yourself out of yourself and that's how your spirituality grows."

"From step one to step twelve it is about helping another human being, so that's always on my mind. I'm going to help another human being. And what's my passion? My passion is now the cold water. My passion is now going into nature."

Kenny began the group after he wanted to share and document his own journey in the cold water. He began to take

"Dip Club's tagline is, 'Where the water is cold, the company warm and the hangover non-existent.' We're a hangover-free social club established by the sea. Founded in October 2022, as a community we prioritise natural highs and alcohol-free socialising. We are ex-London party girls who met on Instagram and began dipping after moving back to the North East.

On a mission to break the stigma on living a sober-curious lifestyle, we began to invite others to dip with us to experience the exhilarating natural highs and human connection that cold water brings."

**Meg Ellis & Katie Scrafton,
Dip Club, Tynemouth**

KENNY'S STORY

I'm a chronic alcoholic. I'm a recovered alcoholic. I don't drink or take drugs anymore. About four weeks before my daughter was born, I had a bad episode – a horrific meltdown. Months before it, my family were all telling me, you need to stop drinking. But I didn't know what an alcoholic was. I knew I was a guy that went to work and drank at night and drank at the weekend and probably took it a bit far – the typical scheme boy, maybe involved in a bit of trouble and drama.

My family kept telling me to stop and I had it in my mind that my daughter was coming in four weeks, and so it's time to stop. But I couldn't. I had no control. As I started to realise that I didn't have any control over my alcoholism, I started to realise, maybe I'm an alcoholic, which is a horrible position to be in, especially for a turning-thirty scheme boy who didn't think he was scared of anything. I started to realise I was scared of everything. I was riddled with fear. I was using drink to mask all this.

What happened then was I went missing for four days, drinking. I self-isolated. I was at rock bottom. After four days of drinking twenty-four/seven, I got myself back up the road, and I was lying in my bed the next morning and I could hear my family all downstairs, all sobbing and sad and upset. I would describe it as listening to my own wake. I was thinking, "Here we go, we're going to get all the alky patter again."

And I had to go down and face it.

There are fifty questions you have to answer for the twelve-step fellowship, to diagnose you as an alcoholic. My sister read them, my mother answered them, and they diagnosed me an alcoholic there and then – and I ended up in the fellowship. I didn't want to do it. I still wasn't sure what an alcoholic was. I went to work every day. I was quite popular. I had a partner, a big house. But at that time, if I put drink into my system, I couldn't stop drinking. And when I wasn't drinking, I was thinking about it. It was a scary place to be.

I went to fellowship, and I met a guy there who was called the Jazz Man, and he was talking about this idea of looking for a power greater than yourself. I was to start praying and meditating and I was to get five beautiful years sober.

Long story short – I did do five years sober. My son was born, my youngest daughter was born, I'd got three children, and although I wasn't with my original partner anymore, I still had my daughter in my life. Everything was going well. I was on the brink of starting a big business in the gas industry. Then we went on holiday. At that time, I'd stopped going to fellowship, stopped working on my programme, stopped everything that was good for me. I didn't realise that my old attitudes and my old ideas of thinking were all slowly trying to creep back into my life again: getting angry, getting aggressive. I wasn't happy with myself. The taxi to the airport was a nightmare, the airport was a nightmare, the plane journey was a nightmare, going to the hotel was a nightmare. The very first morning I went to the shop, pointed up and asked for a bottle. I don't even know where it came from.

Four years later I woke up in hospital after a serious suicide attempt. In that time, I'd built a massive business in the gas industry. I had ten guys working for me. I was getting flown backwards and forwards down to London. But I drank my nights away. I never spoke to my weans, never spoke to my partner. I was isolating in my room every night, getting up in the morning going to work, coming home and drinking till I passed out. That came to a head on Halloween 2021.

I knew twelve-step back to front. But knowledge is irrelevant. Action is everything – and I wasn't putting it into action. So, having a head full of that and a belly full of swally, I was in total meltdown. That Halloween, I couldn't take it anymore and I couldn't stop drinking. I was lost. I had all this knowledge, but I couldn't stop. I had a litre of Morgan's Spice that I'd got as a present when I started my business. I put it all in two big tumblers, and I thought if I drink these two in a oner, I'll never wake up again. So, I gubbed them and woke up in hospital the next morning, thinking, "What has happened?"

I was a lost boy. When the psychologist assessed me, they said, "You know there's nothing we can do for you. There's nothing anyone can do for you. You're as well running back to your meetings." And that's what I did. I went back to my meetings.

I'd already tried the water. About nine months prior, my sponsor from twelve-step took me up into the Campsies in the middle of winter when it was snowing and he put me in the water.

Then, around December, after I had come out of the hospital in October, my big mate said to me, want to try the cold water again? He took me up to the Campsies. I went in and this time I was sober and searching for something. The thing is, with the programme, you're searching for a god of your own understanding, a power you can talk to and hold inside yourself. But being a scheme boy, I was like what is a god? I couldn't understand it. How can I find a god? I don't know nothing about religion.

But when he put me in the water, something came over me. My head went blank. I couldn't think and it was beautiful. I sat in the water and embraced the cold. It was December and freezing, but I was in the zone with it. And I made the decision that day to shut the business down. I paid the guys off and never did another day's work for about four or five months.

In that waterfall, I was searching for a god. I was praying and I was trying my hardest. I was in the water screaming, "Please, God, don't make me drink today!" I was broken. I was at a moment of desperation. In that moment in the water when I felt the cold seeping into me, it came to me like that, *You're going to be alright. You're going to be alright.* Then I started laughing. I was howling to myself. I thought to myself, see, if someone was walking down there and saw me, they'd be saying, "Who is this big bam?" They'd be going, "God save me!"

I came out of the water that day and I felt like I'd been plugged into nature. I'd been plugged into my surroundings, plugged into the cold water, plugged into the deep breathing. And the next morning I woke up and I prayed. I prayed to Mother Nature.

photos and make films of himself, sitting in his whisky barrel out back or up in the Campsies – the Campsie Fells – or at Loch Lomond. "I started turning my camera on and saying, 'Look what's happening everybody.' I felt the craving for alcohol was gone. I've cleared my head and I'm no longer craving it because I'm no longer drinking it."

He made a Facebook page and called it the Polar Bear Club, after a YMCA camp he had helped out at in the United States. "Every morning they did a 'polar bear' – they would take a cabin or two cabins of young boys between ten and fourteen years old to go in the water."

Kenny sometimes described what he went through, and still experiences in the water, as a spiritual experience. "A lot of people get messed up," he said, "with the phrase spiritual experience. They kind of look at you as if you're trying to be some guru. But I do believe that's what I had when I was in the water that day and, having had that, I try to enlarge on it every day. I also think spiritual experience is really just a change of your way of thinking."

Kenny used to run a big business in the gas industry, but he has given that up and now dedicates his time to helping others through cold water. "I'm done chasing money. I'm going to focus on this now. I'm skint and happy!"

The Polar Bear Club page now has 3,600 members, 95 percent of whom are active and watch, like or comment on videos, and Kenny has 10,000 TikTok followers, who tune into his live every morning where he sits and talks "about drink, drugs, recovery and the power of getting uncomfortable". The group, he says, is no longer solely about alcoholics and addicts – but also attracts people with anxiety and depression.

WHERE TO FIND HELP

If you think you have a drug or alcohol problem, often the best first contact is your GP. But help is also available through Alcoholics Anonymous (AA) on 0800 9177 650 and Narcotics Anonymous on 0300 999 1212. AA is there for anyone whose life is or has been affected by someone else's drinking; you can call their confidential helpline on 0800 0086 811.

ICE WOMEN

There is nature – and then there is to-getherness. Both of these matter. Both of these are in the mix when we talk about cold water.

The experience of feeling in sync and at one with others that we felt when we entered the water with the Braid sisters wasn't new to us. Something like it would happen when we swam with our local group, Ice Women, though in a slightly different way.

We would gather on the bank of a small park overlooking the sea and move through standing yoga poses, while gazing out over the water, connecting to the distant horizon. We would breathe together, meditate together, and then we would walk down to the beach.

The group was the brainchild of Colleen Reeve (see Colleen's Story on page 16), who turned to swimming during the pandemic while she was struggling with grief following the death of her father. She talked with us about the importance of moving together as a group. "There's a special connection," she said. "It's almost

like you experience a different sense of self, which transcends the movements. It's a shared thing."

The idea with the yoga class was to create a session in which that synchrony would have a chance to happen, and then the group would immerse and swim in the water, which during the winter in Scotland can present quite a challenge. "Going into the cold water together like that," Colleen said, "it's like you experience adversity together. We're so used to our home comforts, and we're used to going to a normal yoga studio where perhaps you drive to the studio and it's all gorgeous and comfortable and warm; yes, it's lovely, and I still love that. But this is a shared experience of adversity."

What she was interested in was the connection this experience might create. "The more I thought about it, the more I thought that's actually what I want to do – provide that community and that connection."

Someone who inspired Colleen was Laura Hof, daughter of Wim Hof. "I'd read," she said, "an interview in which she talked about how there is quite a bit of machismo around cold water swimming and the Wim Hof cult. There are a lot of men who are very much into Wim Hof, which is brilliant. But then there is also a lot of competitiveness in that culture."

Colleen continued, "But I think what Laura Hof has tried to tap into is a way of taking this space for women, which takes

all of that away and allows people to come and enjoy it just for what it is and nothing more; it's to try to create a network around the world of women who are doing this. That's the concept of the Ice Women community."

THE FIRST OPEN WATER SWIMMING GROUP

All kinds of ideas arise when we talk about what the cold does to us – and many of them don't mention the parasympathetic nervous system, or the sympathetic. Many verge on the spiritual or existential, and that in itself indicates the power of what happens when we immerse ourselves in cold water.

Paul Donnelly, for instance, believes there is something about getting into cold water that brings us into a different state, which he calls unitive consciousness, or "unified" consciousness.

This state of being at one with or feeling at one with all things is what, he thinks, John the Baptist was channelling when he submerged people in the River Jordan.

He joked: "I don't know if they had dry-robes and muffins afterwards, but I've got it on good account that John the Baptist was the actual first-ever cold water group.

"I think," he said, "there's something in the water that can get you to that special state. It's ultimate participation, that's what it is. From an individual point of view, you're no longer spectating or criticising, you're participating."

CHAPTER 6

THE
DAWNSTALKERS

DEDICATED FOLLOWERS OF NATURE

The sun splintered red over the edge of the world. A group of us, idly chatting on Portobello sands, suddenly noticed that crack in the half-light and swivelled. There it was – our old friend – the blushing break of day.

The orb was on the move. It felt as if it was moving towards us, greeting us, inviting us in, and soon we were wading through the water towards it. The waves kicked up, tickling us with cold and laughter. Tossed by the surges, we splashed and danced. The foam-flecked edges burned pink. Skins, reddened by the cold, glowed in the peach of the dawn.

"There's nothing like a sunrise swim," we said.

That morning we were swimming with Swimrise Portobello – but it seemed to us we were also swimming with many others, all the other dippers around the country who had the habit of making immersion in the sunrise their mission. For this is something many of us share – the stalking of the dawn.

That particular Portobello group was

started, during lockdown, by Jo Myles, a hairdresser turned yoga teacher, who came to the water after a cancer diagnosis and treatment.

"For me," she said, "there's something about welcoming in the new day and having that almost spiritual connection with nature. You feel like you're part of nature, not just in it. And the sea has a different character every day. Every day is different. Sometimes peaceful, sometimes more grounded. I became completely mesmerised with the colours, the movement and the light."

She vividly recalled the first sunrise swim she ever did with a group, as if that glowing sun was still rising into view – seared into her memory. "Completely clear," she said, "the sun creeping up, the sky lit up, going more and more golden by the second, breaking over the sea. The sea looked like liquid gold. It was so dreamy. I was feeling so connected. And that was

me hooked. Hook, line and sinker."

During lockdown she began dipping in March and kept going into summer and then onwards. "Basically," she said, "I chased the sunrise as it got earlier and earlier. Just completely fascinated with the light, the movement, the different mornings. This mindset of, I've got another day – another day to celebrate. It was a lovely deep connection to show that gratitude every morning – and to feel part of nature."

That gratitude for each new day, of course, was particularly intense for her. She had only just had a brush with cancer and was coming out of that darkness into the light. "To welcome in the new day," she said. "To welcome the first light. To celebrate getting another chance to live another day. I don't think John the Baptist chucked people in the water for no reason. You come out feeling like you've been completely reborn."

JO MYLES

yoga teacher and founder of Swimrise Portobello

My hope has always been when I share this story that if it can help support one person in a bad situation, it's worth it. Swimming has historically been the love of my life. I'm a Porty girl and grew up close to the beach, so that was my stomping ground as a young kid. My mum and my friend's mum used to drink in the Sands Hotel next to the swimming baths, and we used to be left on the beach, running amok. We could be found singing the *Rocky* theme tune, punching the waves, and generally doing complete nonsense.

Five years ago, my whole world crumbled around me. I'd found a lump in my left breast and found out it was cancer. I'm a single parent. I've got two girls, both of whom were in primary school at the time. It shook my world.

I was told that it was definitely cancer. I had periods of time waiting on results where the world became a very, very dark and scary place. I kept thinking, am I going to be the person who's told that they can't do anything, or that I'm not going to be here for my kids. It was awful. It really was.

But if there's one thing a serious, life-threatening health issue can give you, it's a kick up the arse of your life, and how you're living it. It makes you value every single day, every single breath. Suddenly you don't simply take it all for granted.

It made me look inwards, desperate to make positive changes in my life.

I had this feeling that I wanted to make every day count.

First port of call was being as healthy as I possibly could be: going no alcohol, a plant-based diet, meditating – those are all ways of living that I started. I had to go through two surgeries, a mastectomy, and then a second surgery of lymph node removal. I was offered chemotherapy and radiotherapy, which I took as well.

Those were challenging, difficult times. The chemo was by far the scariest thing. Having your energy zapped, not being able to walk your kids up to school in the morning. But we had a bit of a motto in our house, which was not to forget that this is medicine: good medicine against the dark, unseen, scary thing that you can't really feel.

So fast forward. I got through it and, coming to the end of my treatment, I had this mindset that I was going to get out and live. I remember going on the Sports Warehouse site, and thinking, "Right, I'm going to order us all wetsuits. We're going to be that outdoorsy family."

It's funny now to think I thought I needed a wetsuit to get in the water. When did that happen? I suppose it was because I was being fed images of people with wetsuits ...

The day the wetsuits arrived, we all rushed to try them on. It was a busy weekend, and we still had our food shop for the week to do, so I said, "We'll kill two birds with one stone, we'll go down to the supermarket at Portobello and once we've got our shopping in, we'll jump in the water." I hadn't realised that walking around a supermarket with wetsuits and clothes on top that we'd all be just about passing out with the heat! Ridiculous.

Anyway, we went in the sea. We enjoyed it. We spent some time splashing about. I loved it.

Roll on a few months and we were heading towards winter. I was listening to a podcast on which Wim Hof was speaking as I walked around Arthur's Seat with my dog. The penny dropped. I wanted to try his whole cold water thing.

So, I got in without a wetsuit, I then did the New Year loony dook, and I started doing it regularly. But I was always on my own, so I started trying to find a group. My first group swim was with a group called Wander Women. I loved it — and from there I had a contact, and she invited me to do a dip with a group that happened to be at sunrise. That first group swim was just before lockdown — and I can't be more thankful for that because it kept me anchored for the months to come. In that period, swimming really helped. It helped with focus, with mental health and it gave me a lot of strength. I used to go down every morning. I started in March and took us into the summer — I basically chased the sunrise as it got earlier and earlier. I had this mindset of, I've got another day — another day to celebrate. It was about being able to show that gratitude every morning — and feeling part of nature. I started taking pictures and videos, then editing them to music, trying to catch something.

I remember I was lying in my garden on one of these lockdown days and something popped into my head — oh, you should make a different page for these little videos. So Swimrise Portobello was born. Then I also got the feeling that I'd like to meet new friends. I'd given up alcohol. I wasn't going out anymore. I'll go to a pub, but if you're not drinking and not taking part, you do evolve into wanting to spend time doing other things.

I thought, if I'm feeling like I'd like to meet new friends, there must be others who would appreciate a landing spot to welcome other people. Through that I've connected with some amazing people and built friendships that will last a lifetime.

My life has taken a completely different direction — and swimming has played a huge part in that. I did Pilates training some years ago and I revisited that and started offering Pilates classes at a local church in Portobello, followed by a sea dip. That's now evolved into me completing my yoga teaching training, in which I'm specialising in restorative yoga. I also completed reiki healing. For my next project, I'm collaborating with a fellow swimmer, who is a tapping and meditation coach, in creating Future Proof Retreat, which will offer events and an introduction to wild swimming.

"The swim at sunrise, more than any other time of the day, gives a powerful memory that lingers the longest, evoking the strongest sense of awe, wonder and achievement."

Catriona Yates, Selkies, St Andrews

THE WHEEL TURNS

There's an element to wild swimming that is almost like a nature religion. According to data in the 2021 census, the fastest growing religion in the UK is, in fact, shamanism, another nature spirituality, which has experienced a twelvefold rise in popularity over the course of a decade. Meanwhile, the rise of paganism has also been documented in the United States and the UK. Some attribute this to the climate crisis. Others credit social media, and the rise of "WitchTok" for connecting pagans and spreading their ideas.

But the people we met on our Ripple Effect travels tend to have found their connection more in the seas and rivers than in online spaces. They had, very often, started wild swimming and found something in the water that changed their sense of themselves.

Sasha Udell is one such swimmer. Though she now celebrates the festivals of the pagan calendar in the sea, wears flower crowns and creates her own rituals, her relationship with nature wasn't always like this.

"I'm not a religious person," she said, "and I've never been religious, but I really have a feeling of connection and there is definitely a very spiritual feeling going into the sea, almost like that feeling of awe. You never take it for granted, and it's constantly changing. Even going into the sea on a very calm day, you don't know what it's going to bring – if you're going to have an encounter with a seal or something like that.

"When you go in and the waves are really strong, you know you're going to be bashed about a bit like you're being churned in a washing machine. But you've also got to be wary of currents. There is that feeling of something that's more powerful than you all of the time. I've developed more of a sense of spirituality based on the cycles of nature and the strength of the sea."

For Sasha, at first, swimming wasn't about any sacred connection to nature. When she and some friends started swimming together during lockdown, they would entertain themselves by wearing fancy dress, sometimes with themes, like crochet, or the fifties.

"But gradually what we started to do was move away from the frivolity and focus in on the changing of the seasons," she recalled. "Then we began following the calendar events on the pagan wheel. They began with Imbolc one year and kept on going."

The vernal equinox, Ostara, Beltane,

the summer solstice, Lammas, the autumn equinox, Samhain, the winter solstice . . . The wheel turned, and they turned with it. "It was," Udell said, "marking the points of the year and also the changing of the seasons."

She and her neighbour, Andrea, began to make flower crowns, taking the wreaths they hung on their front doors, and then running round the garden to grab whatever flowers or foliage were there. "Then we pranced down the road together. It felt like a ritual. We would take candles down with us and sometimes fairy lights and we would bring some flowers to decorate the groynes. We were trying to make a nice event out of something simple. Not spending any money – just using things we had. We would wear our flower crowns in the sea. Sometimes we would take flowers into the water and throw them out to the waves."

At the same time, she felt that swimming was helping her handle difficult times and feelings. That connection with the sea was, she said, linked to a need to manage her mental health issues and anxiety. During the pandemic, she was working in a primary school. "It was tough. I feel that the swimming helped me get through that whole period. I'm quite lucky the place where I worked was right next to the beach, so I was going down, having a swim and then going straight into work, still covered in salt and seaweed. Needs must."

FULL MOON RISING

The moon morphed as it rose through the dusk – edges blurred by streaks of clouds. Its gleaming twin was reflected in the sea.

We looked for its line in the water as our feet felt their way through the darkness.

The moon was, I remember saying, our special guest.

I turned fifty in partial lockdown. I'd long been planning a big party and had the local cricket club booked a year in advance. But circumstances were what they were, and instead I had a gathering at the edge of the sea with a couple of friends – and the full moon.

In some ways I couldn't have had a better birthday eve. With that rising lamp in the sky, I felt not alone, but connected – and in a different way than had I held some busy party buzzing with people.

The moon itself felt like a gathering.

It's inevitable that when you start to talk about sea swimming, you also begin to talk about the moon – that great gravitational body that tugs at our oceans and dictates our tides. You begin to talk of spring and neap tides; to time swims according to the tidal cycle. You find yourself buying a moon calendar, checking tidal apps and avoiding the very lowest tides so as not to be faced with a long hike out to still only be knee-high.

Maybe you even start to swim under the full moon.

Among those we met who practised regular group full moon swims was Sarah-Alexandra Teodorescu, an American yogi and shamanic practitioner.

The moon, she said, had always held magic for her. "No matter what phase the moon is in, I am always in awe of her. The moon has taught me so much about honouring and loving every part of my human journey, no matter what phase I find myself in."

Sarah is an example of someone who arrived at the sea already deeply immersed in nature religion but still found something new and intense there – something that heightened the relationship. Her group swims together on key dates and especially on full moons and festivals marking changes in seasons. They drink ceremonial cacao, talk for hours, consult oracle cards, and laugh and journey through all

"We swim daily, we swim at dawn. Dawnstalkers is a call to action, a mindset, a community. Whether at the shore in Penarth or following the same routine elsewhere. Rising early before the rest of world has woken up, doing something hard and out of your comfort zone first thing. The dopamine hit to start your day, sun in your eyes to set your circadian rhythm, grounding, community, connection, joy . . ."

Grant Zehetmayr, Dawnstalkers, Penarth

their emotions. They are four women – Niamh and Rachel from Ireland, Evelyn from Australia and Sarah from the United States – who Sarah described as "chosen sisters".

It was a "life-altering" experience in a Cairn in Orkney that compelled Sarah to move to Scotland. The country, she said, "calls to women". "And then, once you're here, it does not let your heart go." She smiles as she recalls what drew her to Scotland. "The nature, and the nature of the people in Scotland."

"It's incredible," she said, "because none of us are Scottish, but all of us felt this draw, this pull to the land that we couldn't deny. So, we answered, and we keep answering the call of this magical land, and it in return strengthens each of us. Scotland invites and empowers us to become more of our truest selves."

"The first time I went for a cold swim I

joined a wondrous family who I had spent the holidays with in Glencoe. It is part of their yearly tradition to swim in the loch on the first of January. I wasn't sure what to expect, but I knew I wanted to know what it felt like. I trusted them, myself, and the nature around me. It was love at first touch. Everything in my body, especially my heart, was vivid and alive. I felt fully present and fully myself."

She felt, on that dip and each that has followed, as though she was "part of everything". "I felt no separation between the water, the wind, the sun, and I. I was enveloped by everything in nature, and I felt loved, held, supported and so deeply at home in every cell in my body."

Sarah's group frequently swims naked under the rising full moon. She said, "I love being naked in the presence of the women that I love, trust and admire – held, nourished and protected by Scotland's cold and empowering waters. In these moments, there can be nothing but a fully embodied presence."

She described such a moment, which took place in August 2022. "The sky was a vivid and beautiful purple traced with wisps of pale pink clouds. We had made our way into the velvety water right after sunset. The water moved around our bodies, and we could feel each wave as part of the breath patterns of the water surrounding us. I knew in that instant that this was becoming one of those sacred moments that I would return to in memory for the rest of my life. We were all within arm's reach of each other, each individual woman magnificent in herself, and in communion with each other and the whole of nature."

On that same swim, Rachel expressed a desire to float in the sea while being held up by her friends. "All of us," Sarah recalled, "had our fingertips on the back of her body, supporting her as she floated on top of the waves. We each took turns being held by each other. The courage to ask for support when we need it, and to have it offered so open heartedly, is immense. This type of trust is among the things all of us have been teaching each other. We ask for help when we need it. We give it in equal measure. Because, yes, we are each deeply resilient, and yes, we are individually immensely strong, but we are so much more powerful together."

Sarah also runs retreats incorporating cold water swimming. Soul Spas, for widows and widowers, is a particular type of retreat that she co-hosts with a close friend, Ute, in beautiful, nature-based settings around Scotland. Ute began holding these retreats after her fiancé passed away suddenly, and she found that nature was the only thing that helped soothe her grief.

"It's men and women who have lost their life partners coming together to heal in community and in nature," she said. "You can feel grief move through a room like electricity running through it. Grief is shared. The retreats are powerful and deeply empowering. They are definitely the hardest, and most rewarding things I do. It's such a privilege to be there with people who are processing their grief, who feel safe to go through all of their emotions."

WHY CACAO? SARAH-ALEXANDRA TEODORESCU

When I was twenty-eight, my life changed beautifully and irrevocably. I left California and began travelling. I went to Peru to study with shamans. I had incredible, life-altering experiences with different types of plant medicine and felt their wisdom empower me on a molecular level. Ceremonial cacao was one of the sacred plants. Long ago, shamans predicted that when the children of the Earth most needed the healing and power of plant medicine, the plants would answer the call.

Today, cacao expands hearts across the world with the neurotransmitters serotonin and anandamide. The Olmecs called the cacao beans "kakaw" (heart blood) long before the cacao tree was scientifically classified as Theobroma, meaning "food of the gods". Cacao contains the highest amount of magnesium of any food, and is naturally dense with calcium, zinc and iron. As women we crave the nutritional benefits of cacao especially right before our bleed, when our bodies shed and need to replenish their stores of magnesium and iron. The body is infinitely wise in what it urges us to eat, and we need to remember to trust it. The wisdom of the human body craves cacao in its natural form to aid in accessing the power of our emotions, and our desire to connect and create.

EMMIE SCOTT
the Suffolk Circle, Felixstowe

We are a group called the Suffolk Circle. We swim at Felixstowe every weekend for sunrise. We also swim with the full moons and other important dates such as solstices and seasonal changes – most often a skinny dip. We found that by bringing women together in the sea we all felt that connection to become more in tune with the seasons and the world around us.

We are a group of women who are healing ourselves with wild swimming and nature. The cold water brings everyone into the present moment and the conversations that happen are always more meaningful and broaden our connections with each other, which then ripple out into the community as a direct result.

We do this by creating space for women to grow, face fears, empower themselves and each other. By using the simplicity of the sea, we have seen women grow remarkably, and more and more women are seeking us out to join us.

We feel the unique spin on the group is that not only do we want to swim but we also want to help each other to heal. We know the power of the sea; the friendships created around the swim and the water are always deeper and empowering.

The group is going from strength to strength and recently we held a mermaid-themed swim for International Mermaid Day. We dressed as mermaids and had the most wonderful time embracing our inner child. With swim groups like this, it doesn't matter if you start as strangers, because usually by the end of a swim you will end up feeling like you have known each other for years. I believe more than ever that humans are seeking this type of connection, especially women whose relationships can historically be strained into a competitive-style feeling – which is what we want to change. This is a group where the sea and swimming has allowed us to celebrate each other's experiences, and a place for women to feel safe to be themselves without judgement.

SEASONS COME, SEASONS GO

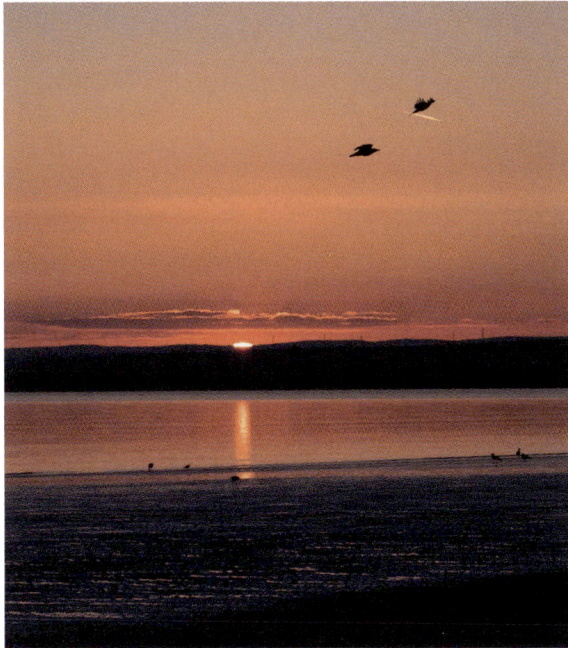

We celebrated Beltane with Sasha. We drank cacao with Sarah.

The wheel of the year turned.

The first time we met Jo Myles of Swimrise Portobello was in the darkness of a winter solstice morning – introduced through friend and fellow-swimmer, Kerrie Flockhart.

As we stood at the shoreline, wreaths were passed around and positioned on heads, clothes discarded, right down to naked, goosebumped skin. We stood in nothing but our crowns and neoprene socks.

The sun was yet to inch over the horizon and the only light came from behind us, the streetlamps of Portobello promenade, and we waded in, anticipating the coming glow, marking the turning point. *Hail the returning light*. We stepped out into the sea's darkness and skinny dipped into the shortest day.

The wheel of the year turned again.

What, I started to wonder, were we doing as we went into the sea to celebrate these moments? What were the feelings we were experiencing about?

AWESTRUCK

One word Sasha used about how she felt whenever she came to the sea was "awe". This word was also used by Michala Harris, a swimmer with the Moon Mermaids of Penarth, as she recollected a swim she did not long after her father died.

"As adults," she said, "rarely are we awestruck. When I think of awe, I think back to one experience when I was in the water – it was not that long after my dad had passed away – and I felt that pull to get into the water and that morning it was properly cloudy, but the sky had opened up, a slither of blue. It was almost like a television set. It's in those little moments where you're awestruck by the beauty of nature and the change in landscapes that you can fully pull yourself into the present moment."

Awe, wonder, even enchantment, are all words that are increasingly being used in the literature around our relationship with nature. Bestselling author Katherine May, for instance, has written that she thinks these moments of awe and mystery are "crucial to our survival".

Psychologists are talking about it, too. American professor (and surfer) Dacher Keltner, in a podcast titled *Wonder and Awe*, described his own reaction to a nature film. He teared up, his jaw dropped, and he got goosebumps. "This awe response and wonder response in our nervous system," he said, "I think dates back to the shift in our evolution some eighty thousand years ago when we started to make art, sing and be together in ceremonial ways."

Professor Keltner has researched what is going on in our brains when we have these feelings – in which we lose our focus on the self and self-interest, and which some describe as like being in touch with the divine.

"The deep thing that happens in the

mind," he explained, "be it in looking at a tide pool or in dancing with a bunch of people at a concert, or in thinking about a big idea that unifies thoughts, is that your mind's narrow focus on itself, self-interest and separateness suddenly dissolves in experiences of awe and wonder. And you feel connected and part of something large – like an ecosystem or a collection of people who are moving together at a sporting event or a dance."

What's all the more remarkable is that Professor Keltner says that when that response happens, and our stress physiology is calmed, our vagus activated, and oxytocin released, we become kinder too.

That's interesting because often when swimmers talked about awe they also spoke of gratitude. Michala Harris, for instance, used the word. "In those silent moments," she said, "where I take myself off to the side, I think about all that I'm grateful for. I try to bring gratitude into that practice too, to be thankful for the present moment and that I get to swim at dawn, and have the ability and capacity to do that."

GIVING BACK TO NATURE

But often in today's world it seems as if the relationship between human beings and the natural world, which we are part of, is broken. These are times of climate anxiety and concern – and that also surfaced frequently in conversations.

If you were to create a Venn diagram of wild swimmers and nature lovers and climate activists, I'm fairly sure you would find a significant overlap between all three, and certainly some of the swimmers we met lived in that space. They spoke of the awe and wonder they feel in the presence of nature – as well as the magic felt in swimming – and using those experiences to make a difference.

Among those is Kerrie Flockhart, a long-time beach cleaner, who is now part of Scottish Coastal Clean Up, a campaign to clear plastic from all of Scotland's coastlines – and who featured in *Taking the Plunge*. I'll always remember joining Kerrie before sunrise on the winter solstice, wearing only wintergreen crowns as we waded into a fairly shallow sea. Hilarious. And glorious.

"It may seem whimsical," she told us, "but these moments are magical and allow for wonderful connection between friends and with nature. The connection I feel with nature while swimming is a huge catalyst for all the beach cleaning I do. It feels like such a privilege to be able to swim in clean waters, yet as a society, we are treating our oceans and waterways so terribly. I would feel uncomfortable about swimming and not trying to do my bit to protect them."

Along with the rise in wild swimming, we've also seen a growing wave of swim activism – often inspired by that heady mix of love of nature and horror at our human impact upon it. Swimming can be a political act – and a group can have political power as well as social magic.

There is, you could say, a bathing waters status movement driven by the horror of sewage in the UK's waters – which is

not just concerned about human health, but also environmental wellbeing. Up and down the country, including in our own Wardie Bay, swimmers have been involved in applications for the status that provides monitoring of waters for harmful sewage-related bacteria. Swimmers against sewage have joined those original water activists, Surfers Against Sewage.

RIGHTS, AS WELL AS RITES

In Scotland, we have a right to roam and the freedom to swim almost anywhere, but in England and Wales there is not the same freedom of access – and swimmers have been coming together to protest this. The biggest of these events is the Great Kinder Swimpass, a mass swim in Kinder reservoir, marking the anniversary of the 1932 mass trespass onto Kinder Scout. In 2023 it saw five hundred swimmers gather to take a dip, defy the law and call for changes, including an English Outdoor Access Code.

So, swimming can be political. Groups can make a mark – and seek to change the relationship in the UK, between people, land, water and power.

Call it divine. Call it what you like. Something happens when we stand before the sea and the sun and the moon. And it touches us. It feels like we were made for it. It feels like we should honour that feeling of being part of it. It feels sometimes as if we should fight for it.

WHY GROUPS MATTER WHEN IT COMES TO CAMPAIGNING

OWEN HAYMAN

founder of Sheffield Outdoor Plungers and campaigner for outdoor swimming access rights

There are two main reasons that outdoor swimming groups are good for swimming access campaigning. The first is that a campaign without a large, vocal, demonstrable following is not going to go anywhere. For people to listen, it has to be a problem that they can't ignore – and you can't ignore thousands of swimmers going in a lake or reservoir or river.

You often need some kind of swimming group to aggregate that community. In some places there will already be swimmers and people campaigning, but the group is needed to share information and to unite and coordinate everyone – to make one coherent campaign. Otherwise, you can have lots of different people all working against each other.

The other benefit of swimming groups is that people with skills, connections and experiences come out of the woodwork, and they are the force of the campaign. It's often just two or three people who know what they're doing and have time to do it – and they will do all the active campaigning work. In our case, it's been four women: Fiona Weir, Imogen Radford, Susie Wheway and Issy Howie, who all have run the water access campaign, speaking to Yorkshire Water about swimming in reservoirs. It's a very slow process, but these four women have patience and find the time when they can.

In a nutshell, a swimming group brings people together, makes a place for the campaign to be centred around so people aren't working against each other – and fantastic people come out of the woodwork who then are the legs of the campaign.

CHAPTER 7

THE
STRIP & DIPPERS

DARING TO BARE

"My goal," said Jenny Massey as we emerged, naked but for neoprene socks, from the swells, "is to be at peace with my body. That's my journey. I might never get there, and I might be really old when I do, but in between I'm not going to stop showing my body."

How we feel about our bodies has a significant impact on how we feel about ourselves. What if swimming naked in a group is an act that can tip us over into some new relationship with our physical selves that could simply make us happier?

What if, in fact, a skinny dip can wash away that tormenting self-critical voice that tells us we're not good enough – and leave us happy in nothing but our own skin?

This was a question we kept asking ourselves every time we went down to the water with some new group of hitherto strangers and began to peel off the layers, strip down to skin and hair, maybe a hat, an HRT patch or a few tattoos.

It was a question in my head one morning when Anna and I found ourselves jumping in and out of the waves with

Jenny Massey and her all-female group, the Perkies, yelping and squealing.

When Jenny, with her friend Angela, first started to encourage other women to join them for a group skinny dip, it was partly about wanting women to be able to feel they could do this thing that seems a little outside the rules. "The main reason I organised the first skinny dip," she recalled, "was because there was a lot of talk locally about a man who used to go in the water skinny dipping, and I noticed how many women were saying that they couldn't do it – couldn't skinny dip."

At first Jenny wasn't sure whether skinny dipping was even legal. But then, when she found out there was no law against people stripping off naked and getting into the water, something clicked for her. "Knowing it was legal and yet hearing women saying, 'I wish I could do that,' was like a red rag to a bull. I said, 'What do you mean? What is actually stopping you? I'll do it with you. I'll get a group together.'"

For her, it seemed like a way for women to reclaim their bodies. "I don't like my body," she said. "I don't like how it looks in the mirror. I don't like how it feels since I had a baby. I don't wake up feeling good in my body anymore. And I used to. I've done races and mixed martial arts and I've felt empowered by being physically active and

strong. But I feel different now. I feel like I occupy more space in my body and my clothes than I want. You can't ignore those feelings. But no one else can criticise my body. I feel quite angry if I think anyone might be judging me. My body is functioning. I made a baby in my forties and now it's going through the menopause. I feel, don't you dare judge me by how it looks!"

The group came up with the name the Perkies. "You know why we chose that name?" Jenny laughed. "Because your tits look amazing in cold water – never perkier!"

At times she has thought about opening up the swim to men. "But it's usually women who are putting more pressure on their bodies – women who have more difficulty with the ways their bodies are constantly changing. Women are continually discriminated against and blamed for what is normal, natural and inevitable. So, I think it's especially important for women and for other people to see women's unfiltered, wobbly bodies in full and glorious motion."

"My swim sisters are the Baps. We stand (and swim) together through thick and thin, proudly tits to the wind on the fringes of the sea in a defiant 'up yours' to the breast cancer that attacked and was defeated by one of us. We all have different relationships with our bodies, which impacts how and where we dip in the nip. For me, I can't wait to get my kit off – whether skinny dipping in the sea at night, jumping naked off a boat, or letting it all out in our local lake, there is pure magic in the contact with the skin. Utter freedom."

Emma Simpson, the Baps, Dip in the Nip

SKIN AND BARE IT

There is always skin – and a lot of it – on display in cold water swimming. You are always, unless you're a wetsuit swimmer, showing a fair bit of flesh. Often, even when you're not skinny dipping, you are a long way towards naked, and yet not quite.

So, it's one small step from wild to skinny, and it's remarkable how many people take it. It's as if there's a logic – particularly among those who have already rejected wetsuits in favour of bathing costumes because of the faff of neoprene – to the conclusion that perhaps the cossie is ultimately unnecessary.

Every skinny dip comes with a sense of risk and transgression. It feels like an act done not quite in secrecy. Getting to know groups that do it felt like entering a secret society – although, actually, it wasn't all that secret. In fact, it's not too difficult to spot these groups on Facebook or other social media. You need only look.

Back in 2019, when we were working on our first book, *Taking the Plunge*, Anna and I found ourselves discussing the fact that we were aware of a fair bit of skinny dipping in the swim community, but we hadn't featured it much yet in the book. So, we decided to set up a group shoot and put out a call for swimmers. We weren't sure very many people would volunteer. We were imagining five or six. But I remember Anna calling to tell me, "You wouldn't believe how many people are saying they want to come."

Thirty doesn't sound like a particularly big number to me now – but it did then, especially when they all turned up at 6.30 a.m. on a June morning, on Wardie Bay, with an Edinburgh city neighbourhood waking up just behind them. Some were regular skinny dippers – others, nervous newbies, keen to try the experience. There was a slight awkwardness as we all stripped off.

When you swim in cold water, you are doing something that takes you out of your comfort zone. But getting naked is, for a great many of us, even more uncomfortable than getting cold. Put the two together and you are pushing through significant boundaries, challenging yourself on multiple discomfort levels.

We were aware of all that on that beach that day, sensing the nerves in the air, before Aster, from the Netherlands, strode boldly down to the water as if she knew exactly what she was doing. Ten minutes later, as we all emerged from the waves, we were hopping around the beach without a care in the world, in spite of the cruise liner passing along the Firth of Forth.

For some people there, that swim was emotionally transformative. One of the swimmers present was psychotherapist Ange Cameron, who had expressed her nervousness before the swim and seemed almost as if she might back out, but by the time she emerged from the water she was jumping around, whooping with joy and keen to have her naked breakthrough immortalised on camera.

She has since talked to me about what that meant to her – and how that started her on a skinny-dipping journey, saying it was all about body power.

"The feeling," she said, "of being naked in the sea is a bigger sense of freedom, calmness, with no sense of judgement or shame and with an all-encompassing acceptance of my being; it made me feel so empowered and at one in my skin. Skinny dipping is so much fun and the moments of joy and carefree elation that I experience in the sea bring a deeper sense of happiness when on land, clothed. When I come out, I feel so invigorated and alive it gives me the confidence and resilience to be with anything that will come my way."

HAPPY LIKE THIS

What Anna and I recall of that morning at Wardie Bay was how nerves dissipated into joy.

That so many people get so much out of skinny dipping suggests that it really is doing something for us. One person who has researched how getting naked together impacts on how we feel about ourselves is Professor Keon West of Goldsmith's University, who is the psychologist behind the television show *Naked Beach*. What he found, which might be surprising to some,

"The feeling of being naked in the sea is a bigger sense of freedom, calmness, with no sense of judgement or shame and with an all-encompassing acceptance of my being; it makes me feel so empowered and at one in my skin."

Ange Cameron

is that, as he writes in a paper titled *Naked and Unashamed*, "more participation in naturist activities predicted greater life satisfaction".

He wrote that such life satisfaction was "mediated by more positive body image, and higher self-esteem". We could call it happiness.

"The take-home message," West said of his research, "is that communal nudity with other regular people (call it nudism or naturism if you like) makes people feel better about their bodies and themselves."

So, if getting naked with other people makes you more satisfied in your life – might stripping off with over a thousand people make you even happier? What we've heard from those who have taken part in some of the UK's biggest naked dips suggests perhaps so.

Those thirty dippers on the beach at Wardie don't sound so many now by comparison with the biggest naked swim that happens in the UK every year, North East Skinny Dip. There, on the long stretch of Druridge Bay, in 2022, a huge crowd

of 1,217 people gathered to strip off and charge into the sea naked, for charity. It's an event that, since the dip started, has raised over £100,000 for mental health charities. Simply by running naked into the North Sea . . .

The woman behind that dip is Jax Higginson, a former paramedic, who revealed to us that the rest of the year she mostly likes dipping alone, just herself and nature, but was inspired by attending a mass skinny dip in the Gower in Wales. "It blew me away," she recalled, "and became an inspiration, to bring a similar event up here. The rest of it sort of evolved over the years. The community grew as well as the appreciation of the mental health connections."

Druridge Bay is an extraordinary seven-mile strip of golden sand, washed by the North Sea. It's partly the scale of this grand sweep, she told us, that makes the experience. "One of the many joys is that we are one tiny dot in the middle of it. We are sort of drowned out by nature. Because we are nothing in nature – even with that many people."

The sheer numbers are part of the magic of the North East Skinny Dip. They electrify the event. "I don't think," Jax said, "that there's a better way to bring energy than a large number of human beings. So, if you add in an early morning and a cold beach and the opportunity to be naked, I think those factors together create so much energy. On the morning of the dip, you feel it – it's palpable on the beach. A lot of it is excitement, but some of it is fear. And it doesn't matter which one it is. We're all pouring our energy into this experience. And then when we run, when we go, give the okay to strip off, it's absolute release. I think that's what it is. I think it's all of us putting the energy together and we don't have access to that when we're alone or in smaller groups."

The feedback after the swims, she told us, was almost always enthusiastic, even ecstatic. People would tell her that they couldn't believe they were able to do it. Or that they couldn't believe how exhilarating or easy it was. Or they would say how it gave them new confidence, or helped to heal from trauma.

"North East Skinny Dip," she told us, "is much more than a skinny dip. It is an experience. A celebration. Of life! Of nature! And of our own, extraordinary, physical bodies! It's about taking a risk and embracing a moment of pure joy and freedom. It provides a rare opportunity to step into our vulnerability, confront shame and smash the beauty myth. It is a unique and healing experience to which every 'body' is welcome!"

NIKKI RANSON

North East Skinny Dip regular and admin for Strip and Dippers

Us swimmers have body imperfections and worry about what people think when you take your clothes off. I got together with my husband in 2009, and when I met him, I would never get undressed in front of him. I'd always go in the bathroom. He'd always say, "You know you don't need to hide yourself, you're beautiful the way you are."

I remember when I first saw the sign for the North East Skinny Dip and I said, "I'm not being funny, but who in their right mind would do that? Absolute complete nutters."

Then in 2017, I was at work and my husband rang up saying, "By the way I've put us forward for the North East Skinny Dip in September. I've paid for the ticket and you're doing it." I was like, what? Really? Why? I was totally gobsmacked, I was scared.

He said, "Look, I have told you from day one that I think your body is lovely."

I was a bit dubious because in 2015 I had a laparoscopy for what turned out to be a problem of endometriosis. After an operation went pear-shaped, I've had tummy flab and scars. I was very self-conscious with them and still am to this day.

I remember going to the dip and I was wearing a Pikachu onesie and when the klaxon went, there's me with my knickers around my ankles trying to tear them off so I wasn't the last person in the sea. Once I'd got in, I looked around at the other people thinking, there's people that are older than me, people who are younger, fatter, skinnier . . . They've got body hair.

But nobody gave a monkey's. When I came out of the water . . . well, I got out of the water saying, "That was amazing. Wow." Why was I scared? I wasn't looking at my body, I was looking at everyone else. Everyone was happy, smiling. People screaming like little kids in the sea. I thought, this is amazing, why have I put myself back for so long?

You see these naked bodies and you think, I'm a part of something bigger. When we went home that day it took me about forty-eight hours to warm up. But I was buzzing. I was full of life.

Skinny dipping is now a big part of my life. I know it sounds a bit cheesy and a bit silly – but it is. I help run a group called the Strip and Dippers.

It took me six years, but I'm now proud of my body, and I don't care who sees it. I was always worried about what people would think. Ooh look at her, skinny with a bit of flab! I sometimes think if I could get rid of my flabby tummy, I'd be happier. But I don't think I would. I think it's part of me now.

IT'S ONLY NATURAL

For some people, however, skinny dipping isn't such a remarkable thing. Perhaps it's something they were raised with, or have got used to doing over the years, almost an everyday event.

Among these is Anna Kotuckova, a member of Edinburgh Skinny Dipping Stories, a group we joined for a clothing-free dip at a reservoir not far outside the city. Anna spent her childhood in Slovakia, and she recalls that seeing naked children by riversides or outdoor swimming pools was normal then. Naturism, she recalled, was not mainstream, but it was "not considered strange either".

"Throughout my life," she said, "I have been skinny dipping wherever I happened to live or visit. I do not see nudity as something which requires any thinking. For me it is simply natural, and it has the added bonus of not having to dry something afterwards. I joined the group to meet more likeminded people who do not make a big deal about something which is primordial. Having a common belief brings together a variety of people. It makes you think, be more open minded and form friendships which otherwise would be highly unlikely to occur."

Skinny dipping for Anna is "just normal" and that was how she described her body too: "normal, nothing special or extraordinary."

PERFECT STRANGER

While some skinny-dipping groups begin with friends devising a plan, others are made up with strangers, who know little of each other when they first reveal all. Such is Edinburgh Skinny Dipping Stories. It began, its founder Lee Simpson told us, with a series of dips with strangers.

Lee had started to swim regularly during the first pandemic summer of 2020, and, when he had dipped his way through his first winter, and hit his first hundred dips, he celebrated with a skinny dip. After he had done a similar celebration on his 150th dip, and the 200th and so on, a Spanish friend encouraged him to set up a group to invite others to join.

So it was that he found himself down at the shore for one of his first organised group skinny dips, with a small group of people, none of whom he had met before. "There was," he wrote in a blog, "a lawyer, an architect, a surfer and an office manager from an insurance firm."

"At one point it felt like I was in some

"I'd been through a lot in recent years – divorce, post-natal depression and depression. I'd lost my tribe. But then I found this new network of people. I'm a bit of an adventurer anyway and I thought, why not? We bond over this. We've all got the commonality. We don't need to worry about anything . . . We know we're all a bit wild inside, and that's something where you can gel with people!"

Caroline Reid, Edinburgh Skinny Dipping Stories

Film4 comedy as it was such an unlikely scenario to be in. To overcome the strangeness of the situation as we finally strolled into the water, I tried to imagine that I was on holiday in Ibiza . . . and was doing this as part of some wild idea to cure a hangover in the early hours."

But, once in, he relaxed and enjoyed every moment of it, and walking back out of the water, he felt there was no sense of unnaturalness. "It felt like we'd all been to the gym and were casually walking from the shower back to the locker room . . . while continuing to blether."

Lee was initially surprised not only at the number of people who quickly signed up to his Facebook group, but also to find so many people willing to turn up to swim when they knew none of the rest of the group. "I thought it was so brave of somebody else to turn up," he said, "with a random stranger, and go skinny dipping. There are more women in the group than men. I take my hat off to all the women who are brave enough to do it – because they've got more on display. It's harder for them to hide everything."

Setting up the group was for Lee Simpson one part of a bigger process – of finding himself and creating a healthy lifestyle. "I'd tried intermittent fasting, veganism, 5km races," he said. "It was a

progression, and this has been the cherry on the cake. It's helped me mentally to be more comfortable and relaxed in society. I think people can get boxed in by what's in the news, but if you get out there and spend time with other people you realise the world's not all you imagined it to be."

He believes skinny dipping has helped him mentally. "I've gone through a transition. I was incredibly shy. When I was taking my clothes off to go for my ordinary dip, I'd be looking around, is there anyone coming this way, anyone coming that way? But in this group, there are none of those feelings. We're all here together. Being together, it's easier."

Lee now thinks what he did in setting up the group, and the release he felt in swimming through the very difficult period of the Covid pandemic, was the opposite of that "midlife crisis" he once thought he might be going through. "Maybe," he told us, "my life crisis has been my whole life? In that I've never felt comfortable – but now I do, because there's more people to socialise with. Maybe what I'm doing now is the opposite of crisis."

CHAPTER 8

YOU'RE WELCOME

FINDING, BUILDING AND CELEBRATING YOUR POD

Not everyone wants to swim in a group. Some want to take to the waters on their own and execute a solo escape and most of us, even in a mass swim, like our moment away from the crowd, communing with ourselves and the sea. But if you picked up this book, we're thinking you're someone who is either in search of swim company or who has already found it – and fallen in love. Call it your tribe, call it your swim family, your swim sisterhood, your pod . . . it's about the togetherness.

We like to call it the pod, inspired by Cairngorms wild swimmer Alice Goodridge, who described to us an early experience of a group distance swim between Mediterranean islands, in which she realised, "I like being part of the pod. It's all about being part of the pod."

It's people like Alice that make the swimming world the marvellous entity it is. She is one of our heroes – not just because of her swimming feats but because of the way she has nurtured a community in Scotland. She does so by bringing the different groups and individuals across the

UK together in gatherings like the Scottish Winter Swimming Championships, Swimwild Winterfest and the Highland Gathering – wonderful, warm, encouraging events that, as Alice would put it herself, are also quite "bonkers".

What's striking is that Alice says the Scottish Winter Swimming Championships are not about the competition. Rather, "It's about getting the community together."

She told us that, from the start, she wanted for the event not to have the seriousness of an International Ice Swimming Championship, but the greater accessibility of the shorter distances advocated by the Winter Swimming Association. It would be about a bit of fun, and maybe even a fancy-dress costume or two. That kind of attitude was taken to its extreme when she introduced the Anything Goes race: where literally anything, including neoprene of all kinds, goes.

"My innocent mind," she told us, "thought the Anything Goes race would be about giving people the option to wear neoprene – for example, neoprene socks or full wetsuits – if they wanted, and, yes, fancy dress is encouraged. That turned into a bit of a free-for-all with the most insanely ridiculous fancy dress the world has ever seen."

The costumes were so wild, in fact, that Alice had to issue guidelines encouraging people to try out their costumes beforehand and make sure they were able to swim in them. "An example of that," she said, "is kilts. They are not very easy to swim in – they become incredibly heavy when they fill up with water. Equally, fake beards can fill up with water and drag your face into the water."

SIX REASONS WHY GROUPS ARE GREAT

by Alice Goodridge

1. They have the knowledge: One of the first things I tell people to do if they ask how to get started with wild swimming is to try and join a local swimming group. There are loads around the UK. The collective local knowledge of those groups and individuals who swim in a particular location is completely invaluable. People who swim in one location, or several locations, regularly will always know the best places to get into the water and have their own routines that you can learn from. If you're starting off it's useful to come along and learn from people. Even if you're not a group kind of person, these informal groups are a great place to start – because you can normally find one or two other people who would be happy to share swims with you.

2. Swimming with a group is safer: It's important that we don't go into the water alone for safety reasons. These groups do provide an important safety aspect as well as a social aspect.

3. They offer encouragement: People in these groups also tend to be really supportive. We're not trying to win any races, we're simply there in the water. We share that love of the water and that connection and that craving of the feeling we get from the water – and also of being around fellow bonkers people.

4. They are a source of friendship: I feel like my swim friendship group has turned into an extended family. I moved up from the south of England nearly ten years ago now and I didn't know anyone up here, and initially I struggled to find people to swim with. I had to set up my own groups. But now I feel like I have an extended family up here, even to the extent that if I don't go down and visit my family over Christmas, I have swimming friends who I can spend Christmas with. Once you've swum together and you've shaken at the side of the loch together and you've looked out for each other, you end up chatting a lot after swims . . . you build a special bond.

5. You're less likely to chicken out: I can be on the side of the loch in the winter and I could easily chicken out of getting in – and that's me, as someone who has swum an ice mile, swum the Channel, swum the length of several Scottish lochs! If I'm on my own, I've got too much going on in my head and my head is telling me not to go in. But if I'm meeting up with a friend or a group for a swim, there's absolutely no question – it's so much easier. Sometimes we sing when we get in. I always make a weird whinnying horse noise when I get in. It's involuntary. There are all those shouts and laughs. It's a real release.

6. It's about looking out for each other: We all keep an eye on each other. Once we've swum with other people, we know the signals as to whether people are happy in the water or they're struggling – and that extends outside the water, too. This is even relevant with people who have only just joined. We had a lady recently who joined us for a swim and then she said she was going to come the next day and she didn't turn up. We didn't know her very well at all but instantly we were worried about her. Someone dropped her a message to see if she was okay. She was absolutely fine. But I think that in an age when people can be quite isolated and detached if they live on their own, then having people look out for you is really nice. Whether it's about safety in the water or as friends.

WHAT ABOUT SETTING UP YOUR OWN GROUP?

If the pod's not there, of course, the other option is to create it. It just takes one person to put an idea out there. Sometimes it's because you can't find a group to swim at the same time, or there isn't already a gang out there meeting each month to howl in the waves under the full moon.

In reality, most groups start up, as you will have seen throughout this book, with someone daring to show up and ask other people to join them. There are many tips for how to do this. You can start a Facebook page, or WhatsApp group, or begin by sharing what you're already doing on Instagram and asking others to join. Then, when you do get together, down by the water, the ultimate key message from those who have done it seems to be to "show up" – be that person who always shows up. And, maybe, bring some drinks and snacks to share.

But you might also want to consider these tips from one expert who really knows how to make groups work and how to welcome new swimmers. Over to Sian Richardson, the founder of the Bluetits.

HOW TO WELCOME NEW SWIMMERS

by Sian Richardson

We get new people coming along every week. A lot of these people will say, "I've been watching you for six months, I didn't come because I thought I was too fat." That's a big one. "My body is revolting, and I didn't think I'd be welcome." So, this is where the posting of the pictures comes in. And I always encourage people to think about if they can post a picture, because people watch the page to see if there's somebody else like them – as tall as them, as fat as them, as old as them, as young as them.

The most important thing is that they've turned up – even if they don't actually swim. We very much push the idea of the Drytit: that it doesn't matter if you don't swim. Just encourage your group to be a community that gathers in the cold or the warm anywhere around water – people don't have to swim. Since we started promoting this, I noticed a lot of people now come to this group I swim in and they say, "I'm a Drytit." They'll always apologise for that. They'll always say, "I'm sorry I'm a Drytit today." I say, "No apologies. And no apologies for wearing a wetsuit. Nobody cares. What we appreciate is that you have turned up."

What goes on in the water stays in the water. But so much goes on in the water. We scream, we shout. This raw human emotion comes out. The cold water is the anchor, the cold water is that thing that provides us with this unlocking of our characters.

It's not only the swimming, it's everything else that goes around it. I love coffee and chat afterwards, so if people run off, I always feel as if I'm hard done by, because I've lost that lovely bit at the end. The water was black last time I went in, and it looked awful. But of course, twenty minutes later we're all sharing biscuits. We're dropping our knickers on the floor, you know, and then the girls started trying to do this jump where you jump up in the air, you click your legs and click your ankles together, and there was laughing, and people were falling over.

I always make a massive, massive effort for the new people in their first couple of weeks. I will always stay in the water until they are out unless there's somebody else who is there. Because I don't want them, when they're initially starting, to feel that they're the first person out.

FORGING A TRULY INCLUSIVE COMMUNITY

The wild swimming community can sometimes seem, from the outside looking in, to be an exclusive club dominated by white women of a certain age. That demographic has changed over time, but it still feels that there's some way to go in making outdoor swimming accessible for all, and we'd love to see that happen.

For us, the question is not just how to find your own pod, but how we can expand it and welcome more people to the swim community and to its benefits – and we were keen to talk to projects that did exactly that.

One of them was Open Minds Active, set up by Maggy Blagrove and Wafa Suliman, around making swimming accessible to women of colour, refugees and asylum seekers in Bristol.

Wafa is a former professional swimmer from Sudan who struggled to access swimming when she arrived in the UK – and who had a love of getting more women into swimming, especially adults, who have not had the opportunity.

She said: "So many women in our community have never been given the opportunity to swim, despite living in the UK a long time. The sessions are more than just swimming: we support each other and encourage generations of women from within the same family to do something for themselves."

We spoke with Maggy, who comes from a background in using sport, previously netball, for social change and had observed the lack of diversity in outdoor swimming, which she thought "a shame because it's such a welcoming, inclusive community".

"It has been really powerful," she told us, "working with Wafa as a Muslim woman representative of those communities, making that contact and being that role model, saying, 'You can do this.'"

If we want to diversify open water swimming, Maggy said, we have to take several steps back. "We have to first look at the barriers to swimming in general, and that was where we started. We'd been talking with women, mostly from the Somali community, plus a few of Wafa's Sudanese friends who had settled here in the UK but didn't feel that connected. They didn't feel welcome at a lot of leisure centres, and so we decided to create a women-only space."

Maggy recalled talking with a group of Somali women about the idea of running a swimming programme. "I said, why wouldn't you want to come and swim? And they laughed and said, a lot of us can't swim, and often we don't feel welcome or safe at public pools. So, I thought, okay, that is an issue."

She and Wafa tried twenty-seven pools

in Bristol and found only one that could accommodate them. Eventually they started the programme as the UK emerged from the pandemic lockdowns, in a learning pool with the blinds pulled down, with twelve women. They have, at time of writing this book, now taught over a hundred.

Having learned in the pool, some of these women progressed to the lake – a small inland body of water, recently taken over by a new owner, chosen because it wasn't too deep, and crucially wasn't too public or overlooked. The owner agreed a two-hour safe space once a week for the women.

Wafa observed: "It was the first time many of the women swam outside on our outdoor women of colour session. It has been lifechanging for them."

And, Maggy said, not everyone who got involved swam – but that didn't matter. "Being outside in nature was enough for some of the women. Some came along and watched, held the baby – and others got in the water. It was intergenerational. We had a granny from Pakistan, who hadn't been in the water since she was a teenager. The granddaughter she brought along had never seen her granny swim, she didn't even know she could swim, and she couldn't swim herself."

Having witnessed the powerful

experiences and feelings going on in the water, Maggy quickly also noticed how much it seemed to be helping these women, asylum seekers and refugees who felt incredibly isolated, to feel a connection with Bristol and with each other.

Wafa, too, saw how this transformation was working on multiple levels. "I am always getting messages from husbands," she observed, "saying how much happier their wives are since they have been swimming with us. The WhatsApp group the day before the session is full of women messaging about how they are looking forward to the session, they get really excited each week, which is so great.

"The women say learning to swim has given them confidence and it's time for just them, away from the kids and the stresses of life. It gives me a good feeling too, being able to make this happen for other women like me and creating a community where we laugh and support each other."

Open Minds Active now run various programmes, from pool and open water swimming for refugees and asylum seekers, to social-prescribing initiatives involving cold water swimming for any woman referred with mental health issues or long-term health conditions. This year, 2023, their two-hour weekly sessions will likely bring around sixty women to the water.

Among the barriers for many of the women, Maggy observed, was dress. But the group found ways round that. Orca donated wetsuits. Finisterre brought out a sea-suit and donated some. "But," Maggy said, "the women themselves come up with their own solutions. There have been some amazing homemade swimming outfits."

The most important thing, however, was having a safe, welcoming space. "It was about the women being with people who they trust and who they knew would look after them, because it can be scary. We speak to refugee families who have been told, 'Don't go near the water.' Some are dealing with severe trauma associated with water on a number of levels. This could be caused by a negative experience in childhood, involving a boat crossing or simply having no knowledge of general water safety."

Open Minds Active are now training some of the women as peer mentors and facilitating others to work towards their swimming teacher qualifications.

"It's more than just swimming," Maggy said. "We run workshops around women's health, signpost to different services and support, plus we connect with other organisations who provide other nature-based activities like walking and running. The friendships build confidence and encourage a sense of adventure and willingness to try new things. Plus, engaging the women has a ripple effect, felt not only within their immediate families, but also the wider community. As they have conquered their own fear of water, many of the women swim regularly with their children, which they didn't before. We now are receiving a lot of requests from men to learn to swim, as they've seen first-hand the benefit swimming has had on their family's wellbeing."

LOUISE
swimmer with Open Minds Active

I have severe depression and, while the medication is effective, it leaves you numb and emotionless. When I'm in the water, my mood feels lighter, and a feeling of peace descends over me, and feelings start to come back. For me, this lasts until the next day, and I feel human again. The community and support from the other ladies is wonderful.

MEHBOOBA
swimmer with Open Minds Active

Cold water has helped me to manage my fibromyalgia. I experience severe body aches and it is very debilitating, but on the days I cold water swim I feel better, and I am more energetic. The most valuable thing about it is that it makes you feel like you are a part of nature, it is so soothing. I am now swimming twice a week whereas I was doing nothing before. I really want to try and swim all winter now!

HOW TO MAKE IT EASIER FOR OTHERS TO JOIN

by Rachel Ashe

At Mental Health Swims, we try to think: what modifications do we need as individuals to make it okay to be part of a group? I want to make it easier for people to ask for those modifications that they need.

I need lots of clear instructions. I'm not very good at reading between the lines. Sometimes I need to know exactly what's going to happen. So, our training emphasises that.

We're very careful about photos and videos. For somebody who lives with body dysmorphia, or social anxiety generally, or has low self-esteem and body confidence, we're very careful about taking photos. We do an opt-in where, rather than just being told, "If you don't want to be in a photo, step out now," we say instead, "We're gonna take a photo over here. You want to be in the photo? You're very welcome."

It's the same for food. In the swimming community, we love cake, but there are people who come to our swim groups who have issues with food, and they don't want to feel that it's something that is pushed on them. So, again it's a reminder that that's not for everyone, and we don't need to push the point.

We make it clear that if you have access issues for whatever reason to get in touch with us beforehand, so that we can come up with a plan together.

We also don't pressure anyone to actually get in the water. You can come along and dip a toe. You can come along and have a splash, or you can just come along. There's never any pressure, and the same goes for clothes. Just come in whatever feels okay for you. And if that's leggings and a T-shirt, that's fine.

We ask that our volunteers don't make any assumptions. I think that's the other thing, not making assumptions about someone's gender or their home situation – simple things like that, which can make a place feel safer.

THE WONDERFUL WORLD OF SWIM GROUPS

There are thousands of groups around the UK, so there's no chance of us offering a definitive list here – but we thought we'd introduce you to a few of our favourites and let them tell their stories.

CHRIS COWMAN

Take the Plunge, Surrey, @taketheplunge_

Starting on an icy morning in Dec 2021, me and a good mate kicked off a cold water charity challenge for MND. Our band of brothers has grown as we have invited more to join the experience and enthusiastic word-of-mouth continues to spread. We plunge every Friday morning at sunrise.

CHRIS NICHOLAS

Ice Guys North East, Tyneside, Northumberland and Ayrshire, @iceguyscic

We copied the lasses! Wild Sea Women started in Sunderland in June 2020 and a few of their partners asked if there was a men's group. There wasn't, so they suggested I set one up. Swimming with people from the community has been fantastic for making likeminded new friends and building a support network for men in the area. We've connected with other groups around the country and set up another three Ice Guys groups in Tyneside, Northumberland and Ayrshire.

The atmosphere at our swims is always positive and a lot of people have said it's a cornerstone of how they keep their mental health in good shape. If we do nothing else, that's good enough for me.

EMMA WILLIAMSON
Selkies, Shetland,
@Shetlandswimmerselkie

I swim in Shetland and we have a local group on Facebook, which I set up number of years ago, called Selkies. It was set up as a community group for all swimmers, but also for those visiting Shetland. Now I dip in and out of groups of swimmers here, visitors often come with me too, and I love to swim alone as well.

I also did some fundraising swims to raise money for charity as my friend's son has a brain tumour. I find that if you feel hopeless, the sea shares the burden. I continue as it keeps me immersed in my natural environment, which grounds me. It's a gift that means I can go anywhere anytime with no kit and just swim if I feel like it.

PIPPA RENYARD
Salty Sisters Porthleven, Cornwall,
@saltysistersporthleven

Our group name is the Salty Sisters, we were founded in 2019 and have grown from one member to about 150 at present! We're based in the fishing village of Porthleven in the far southwest of Cornwall and swim enthusiastically all year round. Our story began when I started swimming solo, and my mantra became "I'll keep doing this so long as I'm having fun and enjoying it" – and I just didn't stop! Bit by bit, people joined me, and we've now become the closest of friends and have so many memories we share. We've held two big charity swim events, connected with the local arts festival, shot and launched a short film, and hosted several parties and weekends away. Many of our group have

found that swimming has "saved" them in some way – and this has become a very real part of the salty "glue" that keeps us together.

FRAN WADDINGTON

The Blue Flamingo Swimming Group, North Yorkshire, @franrosewaddington

When I found my swimming group, I found my tribe; these women and the icy cold water have, without meaning to, helped me heal from fertility heartache and the ensuing crisis this meant for my life. We swim weekly and we are also taking part in a challenge – to swim thirteen full moons this year.

DEBBIE BLACK

Black Sibs Group, Aberdour Black Sands

I discovered wild swimming in lockdown. Three of my five siblings started shortly after: Laura, Jenni and Charles. We lost both our parents in 2021 – Mum in March to Alzheimer's and Dad in December to cancer – and we found wild swimming has really saved us. It has helped us with our grief; I've recently been diagnosed as bipolar too – so it also helps with that. And it has created a bonding activity for us siblings. Mum's ashes are scattered at Black Sands, Aberdour. We get together at Black Sands and swim on Mother's Day, special birthdays and random days to all swim together. It's so special to us as a group, and to our children too.

DEBORAH PRICE
The Permanent Waves, Hove

We are about ten regular swimmers and we started up during lockdown, as it was a way to see each other at a distance. We swam, or dipped in my case, all that summer and through the winter and have kept up ever since. For one birthday, on a cold April morning, we all wore sarongs and did a dance routine to salsa music then ripped the sarongs off and ran into the sea! We've learned to read the sea and tides. I've discarded my wetsuit as the humiliation of struggling in and out of it wasn't worth it. The swimming is a huge part of my life now and something that I'm so proud of it.

FIONA HUNTER
Cairngorm Wild Swimmers & Ice Women, the Highlands and Edinburgh

My first Wild Swim was led by Alice in June 2017 at Lochandorb. It was blowing a gale and I swam with the group who had all come for a "taster", to the island, where we wandered before returning. My hands turned to claws halfway back; I had no idea it was a sign of hypothermia! The photo shows quite how high I was at having survived – I was buzzing! Then we all went for coffee and within minutes I realised I had found my tribe. Soon after that I joined the Cairngorm Wild Swimmers and the Wild Ones in Edinburgh. When north, I went to the regular swim at Loch Morlich on a Sunday morning and, in Edinburgh, I usually went to Wardie on a Sunday afternoon.

KATIE HAWKINS
Friday Swim Club, Edinburgh

Originally formed by my friend Kerry to help Bryony make her fifty different swim spots before she turned fifty, Kerry asked me if I wanted to join so I could get into sea swimming. What it has then done is create a beautiful bond with two other incredible women who inspire me each time we meet and support me no matter what. On days when I've really struggled and cried, had difficulty breathing, they have both been incredible. We have also added to our swims with a litter pick before the dip and then a breakfast of overnight oats and a chat afterwards. Our chats in the sea are filled with laughter, silliness and giggles and deep unveiling of layers as well. I bloody love these women and what open water swimming has brought to me through them.

JAMIE CRAIG-GENTLES & CAROLINE BLAIR
Bob and a Blether, St Andrews, Fife, @bobandablether

It started with two mums bobbing about and having a blether in the North Sea, on the breathtakingly bonnie shores of St Andrews and of Elie in Fife. Today, it has evolved into a wonderful collective of women who enjoy time together in the water and raise money for charities on dry land. There's a great saying that you can't pour from an empty cup and Bob and a Blether is our way of filling that cup. We, as women, wear so many hats (boss, mum, employee, wife, student, daughter . . .

daughter-in-law), but it's when we wear our bobble hats that all of our other roles and responsibilities float away, and we can focus solely on ourselves.

CLAIRE WALKER

Lake Swimming Ladies, Windermere, Lake District, @lakeswimmingladies

After starting and renewing my love of swimming a few months earlier, it was in November 2019 that I decided I needed to help others who, like me, were a little lost, in pain from various ailments or, also like me, lacking in total confidence in everything!

The swim community I joined from our local village ignited something in me I'd forgotten I had and so @lakeswimmingladies was created via an Instagram account after a gin and tonic or two . . .

Little did I know that I would be even more inspired by the wonderful women and men that I've met and grown to call my swim family. The ages of our swim community range from those in their early twenties right up to the over seventies, from all walks of life, so there's never a dull moment!

CATH BROWN

Salty Seabirds, Brighton

We are the Salty Seabirds and swim all along the coast in Brighton and Hove. We are open to all – the name misleads that it is just for "birds"! – and strive to be welcoming and inclusive to encourage more people to come along for a dip, a swim or a chat and a biscuit on the beach. Our swim group began as a spin-off from the Seabirds social enterprise that, among other activities, runs free swimming lessons for local refugee women – and our members volunteer in the water to support these classes. We have started our own winter swimming challenge – the Arctic Tern – that helps fundraise for this, too. We meet for moon swims by our West Pier, we mark International Women's Day and other occasions, and we ran "fur coat no knickers" swims in lockdown for members to glam up to get in the water and give each other a laugh.

HELENA GRACE

Salty Grief Warriors, Hove

When my son died suddenly in March 2022, it felt like nothing, and no one, could even touch the edges of the unrelenting pain. I had swum periodically over the summer but never through the winter. By November of that year, something called me to the winter sea and there I experienced a tiny moment of relief. I felt connected to the vast primal forces of nature. The pain of the cold was a relief from the pain of grief. I was so grateful for that tiny moment. I began going weekly as a tribute to my son and for my own physical and mental health. I felt he was with me and cheering me on. At the time, I also felt isolated and, if I'm honest, a bit mad, despite the unbelievable support of friends and family. I needed a tribe. With some trepidation, I approached Salty Seabirds and, with their support and encouragement, I did a shout-out on the Salty Seabirds Facebook page to see if any other bereaved parents

were interested in joining me. Slowly, people started to connect, and the Salty Grief Warriors group was formed.

Salty Grief Warriors is a small peer-support sea swimming group for bereaved parents of older and adult children. We meet monthly for a couple of hours, usually on Hove or Shoreham beach. We dip if we feel like it and we talk if we want to. When we swim, we feel empowered and proud of our courage in a situation where disempowerment, shame and guilt is common.

When we talk, we know that we are talking to others who will not judge us, who understand and have our backs – on the beach and off. We have introduced a short practice of listening deeply to each other without advice or comment, as we know that listening is the gift, not words. We dedicate our swims to our children. In the sea we can laugh or cry, howl or be silent, share our strength and our pain. Swimming has given us a purpose and a bond, across all ages and backgrounds. Together we have created something profound and, for some of us, life changing.

JULIE NIMMO & GREG HEMPHILL

Soulful Sunday, Luss

Greg and I have been attending Natalie Valenti's Soulful Sunday yoga and dipping group at Luss Beach for the best part of two years. To say it's been life changing is an understatement. When I first went, there were eight of us there. Last week there were nearly seventy. It is such a warm and welcoming group. Natalie leads us in breathwork and gives us the focus to get in that water. We've met so many new people. New pals, first timers looking to try something new and likeminded folk. One of the things we love is, after a dip, sitting

in our dry clothes having a cup of tea and a biscuit round the fire, chatting and listening to Natalie's husband David playing the guitar and singing his songs.

When you come out of the water, your brain and body are firing on all cylinders. It's an amazing sensation and an incredible start to a Sunday morning. We always leave with a smile on our faces. It's so cool to have found a new tribe. I love it so much that I am now training to be a yoga and cold-water dipping teacher with Natalie.

ISLAY HERRICK

The Barean Swimmers, Galloway

The Barean Swimmers came together as a group during all the Covid shenanigans. We were friends, friends of friends and newly moved to the area. From a core of four we've grown to around forty members, some yet to dip their toes in the water, others dook daily. Ages range from teens to seventies.

The companionship the group has given is immeasurable.

We are all grateful to live in Galloway with coves, sandy beaches, quiet lochs, waterfalls and rivers on our doorstep. It is beautiful.

NICOLA WILKINSON

Wild Swimming Caldervalley, @wild_swimming_caldervalley

I started wild swimming alone and then I would occasionally invite small groups of people to share my absolute love and passion for it. This eventually grew when I became more confident in organising

larger groups and the rest, as they say, is history!

Community has become such a huge part of my wild swimming journey and each group swim I organise is bigger than the one before it. I organise group swims once a month and for momentous occasions such as International Women's Day, full moons and the summer and winter solstices.

Whether there's a turnout of thirty or a small handful at the group swims, each swim is unique in that they bring together the most amazing people and no swim is ever the same. We share life lessons, belly laughs, tears, raw and unfiltered emotion. There is something so unforgiving and

special about being in or near that water that seems to give people permission to let go and be nothing but themselves. It's pure magic.

PIPPA BEST

Out of Sink Synchro Swimmers, Penzance, @outofsink8

Mary Woodvine had the idea to get the nine of us together to try synchronised sea swimming in 2021, in the lead-up to COP26. Half of us were already regular or semi-regular sea swimmers, but the rest were relatively new to cold water swimming. At first, we thought it would be a fun incentive to get in the water more

often. But as we're all passionate about protecting the planet, especially the sea, we quickly realised that we could also use synchro to bring attention to environmental issues: eco-synchro! We chose the name Out of Sink to reflect that intention – but also to keep expectations reassuringly low . . .

At our very first meeting, we decided to give ourselves a mere six weeks in which to become a team and learn a synchro routine, ready to perform to the public in Jubilee Pool, our local Art Deco lido. To raise awareness of the impact of rising tides and the climate emergency, we planned to perform the routine on land, too – "synchroing" our way from Newlyn to Penzance, and linking up with protests all over the world.

We practised on land, in the sea, in the lido and at our local leisure centre. When we finally performed, the mistakes only made it more hilarious, and mostly we were genuinely synchronised – it was brilliant! Best of all, it brought the community together to learn more about the threats to coastal communities like ours – and the experiences of others already suffering the impacts of climate change all around the world. And, by coming together to do something difficult in very little time, we were able to remind people that we can all make a difference, and that having a go now, imperfectly, is always better than doing nothing.

LAURA THOMSON & JOANNE GORDON
Wild Swimmin Wimmin, East Lothian

We started our swim adventure during lockdown in winter 2021; as besties, we needed a reason to get out and see each other regularly. Most of our friends thought we were mad! But once they heard our stories of how amazing the cold water was making us feel – not to mention the improvement in certain menopause symptoms – a few other brave souls donned their swimsuits and joined in our journey. There was now five of us, including my thirteen-year-old daughter, throwing ourselves into the big blue and so Wild Swimmin Wimmin was born.

SHELLEY SIM
Salty Sisters, Dunbar

What I love about wild swimming is how you get to just "be". It doesn't matter what you do or where you are from, you are just being. You are being yourself and being fully in the moment and sharing that amazing experience with other individuals, who are also just being themselves in the moment. It's a pretty special experience.

AFTERWORD

WE ALL SWIM TOGETHER!

Bonkers, they say. That word comes up again and again. Mad as a box of frogs, said Sian Richardson. All of which is a reminder that there is some kind of distinct character to wild swimming culture – which perhaps stems from the fact that getting into cold water seems, to most, a little bit daft.

But, of course, most of us who do it no longer see it as madness at all. It's the opposite. It's what helps keep us mentally well. And doing it together, in company, is a key part of the spell.

It seems like stating the obvious to say that people like to come together to do things, which is, essentially, the story of this book – but it does feel like it needs to be restated in these post-pandemic times.

This book is a celebration of that magic that happens when we get in the water together. It came out of our marvelling at the welcome we found in the groups we kept coming across, just as we did our other books. The swim community is like a giant family whose arms stretch out, with relatives dotted all around our coasts and waterways.

The wave keeps on growing and the family keeps on expanding – and we hope this book inspires you to expand it more. What's fascinating is to explore what so many groups share, what they have in common. They're fun, welcoming, silly and, as much as they're about the cold, they're also about a warm hug and the occasional moonlit swim.

Merfolk, selkies, tits and balls, blue or any colour. All are welcome in the water.

We hope to see you there.

THE SAFE DIPPING CODE

This book, *The Ripple Effect*, is all about fun and togetherness, but let's not forget that entering open water is a risky activity. Wherever you swim, whoever you're with and however experienced you are, we recommend you stick to the following code. Stay safe and have fun!

1. Don't drink, or take drugs, and swim – in other words, always swim sober and remember how even small amounts of alcohol can impair your judgement.

2. If you're looking to try a new swimming spot, source local knowledge on where it is safe to go and if particular locations have any risks.

3. Make sure you have an exit point.

4. Check for risks like rip currents or river rapids.

5. Be aware of your own limits. Just because someone thinks they can swim to the other side of the loch, doesn't mean you can.

6. Be aware of the weather and tide times. Check the forecast so you're aware of what you may be dealing with; also, if you are sea swimming, the tides. If it's been raining recently, you should be aware that rivers and waterfalls will be in spate, and faster running, and that there may be more sewage, which has been allowed to outflow, in rivers and the sea.

7. Remember that water can suddenly get deeper. What can seem like a shallow entry can suddenly shelve off.

8. Don't jump or dive in until you have done a thorough risk assessment and know the water is deep enough and clear of obstructions.

9. Don't try to rescue people in trouble. Raise the alarm at once. Dial 999 or 112 and ask for the Coastguard, or relevant agency, to ensure trained professional rescue services are on their way. Throw something that floats into the water, if possible, to help them, or tell them to simply float, rather than swim.

10. Watch children at all times.

11. Swim parallel to the shore rather than away from it.

12. Avoid swimming close to weirs: the area at the bottom of the falls can trap swimmers and hold them under the water.

13. Allow yourself to be seen. Wear a bright swim cap or use a tow float.

WHAT YOU REALLY OUGHT TO KNOW ABOUT COLD

1. Cold water shock

Among the dangers of cold water swimming is the shock your body goes into the moment it is immersed in the cold.

"Even in summer months the water in the UK is cold," says coach Sarah Wiseman. "Cold water shock is caused by sudden immersion in cold water and can be triggered in water temperatures below 15°C. The sudden cooling of your skin can cause you to gasp involuntarily. Your breathing rate can change uncontrollably and significantly increase. These responses can contribute to feelings of panic and to inhaling water into the lungs directly. This can happen quickly. Cold water shock can also increase the heartrate, and this can increase the chances of a heart attack. If you have any concerns do check with your GP before you take the plunge. Many people die following sudden cold water immersion each year. Don't dive or jump suddenly into cold water, and if you do find yourself struggling with cold water shock, then please do follow the RNLI advice to float for around sixty to ninety seconds. This is the time it takes for the effects of the cold shock to pass and for you to regain control of your breathing."

2. Afterdrop

Almost all of us swimmers have felt it. You get out of the water and you're feeling good – feels like you're stoked by a fire inside! – and then, before long, the cold hits and suddenly you're chilled, shivery – on the road, you fear, towards hypothermia. That's afterdrop: your body's continuing fall in temperature that goes on long after you've left the water. While you were in there your body constricted the blood vessels in your extremities, keeping warm blood in your vital organs, but once you're out of the water the vessels dilate, cooling the blood that runs through it and onwards to your core. Needless to say, this can be extremely dangerous – and lead to hypothermia.

3. Hypothermia

Hypothermia is defined medically as a core body temperature of below 35°C. It creeps up on you gradually. Hypothermia slows your thought processes down, so before you swim it's a good idea to set your clothes out in the order in which you will put them on when you get out. Have your towel ready and at the top of the pile.

SARAH WISEMAN'S GUIDE TO THE SIGNS OF HYPOTHERMIA

- Loss of coordination.
- Changes in your swimming stroke – your body position may become more vertical in the water.
- Arms and legs may feel heavy, numb, or sluggish.
- Uncontrollable shivering and numbness in the body.
- Clenched jaw and difficulty speaking.
- Hands becoming claw-like and less ability to control them.
- A feeling of elation and happiness

WHAT TO DO IF YOU ARE EXPERIENCING HYPOTHERMIA

- Get out of the water immediately.
- Remove ALL wet clothes as soon as you can.
- If possible, find some shelter or somewhere warm.
- Stay out of the wind if it is windy.
- Don't rub your skin to dry – pat it.
- Layer up in warm, dry clothing, including hat, gloves and warm socks.
- Drink something warm and some food. NOT alcohol or caffeine.
- Do not use a shower or bath for somebody who is hypothermic.
- Let your body shiver.
- Use a hot water bottle. NOT directly next to the skin – wrap it up in a towel.
- Last but not least, do NOT drive until you are certain it is safe to do so, or ask somebody else to drive you.

For more information on water safety see www.outdoorswimmingsociety.com, which has published a host of guides and articles on the subject.

ABOUT THE AUTHORS

Vicky and Anna have been swimming together since 2018 when a mutual friend introduced them, saying, "You two both like wild swimming, maybe you should even write a book together". Within a year they had travelled the country, going on swim safaris, plunging into waterfalls and dipping in bays with some of the remarkable swimmers featured in *Taking the Plunge*. And they didn't stop swimming and writing there. They drew together the hive mind knowledge of the swim world in their *The Art of Wild Swimming* guides to Scotland, England & Wales and Ireland.

All the way through they have been dipping away with their own local groups, big and small, and marvelling at the joy and support swimming with others can bring. But it was a dip with a community in Ireland called the Ripple Effect that inspired this book and its title. From then on they started to see ripples of infectious love everywhere. They wanted to spread the news, to turn those ripples into words and images and put them out onto the ocean as a book.

Vicky Allan is a journalist who writes chiefly about the environment (and especially watery issues) for the *Glasgow Herald*. She is also the author of a book about the menopause, co-authored with television star Kaye Adams, titled *Still Hot!* and a creepy cat novel, *Stray*.

Anna Deacon is a photographer and writer who has also written a popular travel guide book titled *Wild Guide Balearic Islands* with her sister Lizzie, and published articles for *The Guardian*, *Scotsman* and many more. She also hosts the popular Instagram page @wildswimmingstories from which these books began.

ACKNOWLEDGEMENTS

Thanks to all the groups that have welcomed us, both whilst working on this book and throughout our swim lives.

To the swimmers who wrapped us in their warm hugs, held us tight, and inspired us.

To all the dippers of Wardie Bay, and especially the Wardie Bay Original Gangstas.

To The Ripple Effect's Mandy, in Ireland, for sparking our imagination with a name.

To Gilly McArthur, Alice Goodridge, Mark Harper, Rachel Ashe, Fenwick Ridley and all our other swim heroes.

To all at Black & White for encouraging us to write about wild swimming again. Not just another book, but another adventure.

To Fiona Atherton, for helping us to spread the ripple.

To our families, for putting up with us heading off to the water again.

To the sea, and other precious waters, that give our swim communities a home.